YOUNG VOICES

AN ANTHOLOGY OF POETRY
BY NASSAU COUNTY STUDENTS

YOUNG VOICES

AN ANTHOLOGY OF POETRY
BY NASSAU COUNTY STUDENTS

Dear Emily ~
I'm as proud of you
now as I was in 2009
(p 154-155). :) Go for it all!
xo, Judy 7/2014

PRESENTED BY:

Maxwell Corydon Wheat, Jr.
Nassau County Poet Laureate

EDITED BY:

Judy Turek

Allbook Books

Selden, NY, USA

The poems contained in this book were submitted by Nassau County students to the Nassau County Poet Laureate School Poetry Contest and judged by a panel of poets for placement in this book.

Cover Design by Joseph Camacho.

Text is printed with soy-based non-petroleum ink on 100% recycled and FSC (Forest Stewardship Council) certified paper which is processed chlorine free. Front and back covers are printed on FSC certified paper.
For more information visit:
www.fsc.org
www.rainforest-alliance.org
www.environmentalbychoice.com
www.bookprinters.com/marketing/environ.html

Recycled
Supporting responsible use
of forest resources
FSC   www.fsc.org Cert no. SW-COC-002283
© 1996 Forest Stewardship Council

Printed in the United States of America.

Published by: Allbook Books
                PO Box 562
                Selden, NY 11784
                www.allbook-books.com

ISBN-10: 0-9818661-3-1
ISBN-13: 978-0-9818661-3-0

FOREWORD

I'm proud to present *Young Voices, An Anthology of Poetry by Nassau County Students*.

The poems in *Young Voices* were submitted to the Nassau County Poet Laureate School Poetry Contest by Nassau County school students. *Young Voices* is the result of the best poems from each grade, Kindergarten through 12th Grade. The book features the top three poems, Gold, Silver, and Bronze and 12 Honorable Mentions per grade. All of the poems received were read and judged by a panel of poets.

As a lifelong poet, I am impressed by the quality and diversity of the poems produced from the school system in Nassau County. Each poem contains elements of surprise, in-depth sentiment, excitement, or a determination to elicit change, whether personal or global, with a passion for words. Congratulations to our next generation of poets!

These students have proved that language is the flow of words that reach out to the reader, based on their creativity, experiences and insights, whether utilizing humor or intense emotion. Fresh language, inspirational combinations of words, and use of poetic tools have created this extraordinary volume of poetry.

I want to extend my gratitude to all of the students for participating in the contest, to school districts, and to all school personnel for their encouragement to students to write poetry that is meaningful and vivid literature. In addition, I extend my sincere thanks to our sponsors and my committee for their labors throughout this endeavor to publish an outstanding spectrum of poets in *Young Voices*.

I am indebted to Judy Turek for chairing the project, her dedication in organizing the contest, and editing this book.

I hope you will enjoy the artistic talents of Nassau County students in *Young Voices*.

Maxwell Corydon Wheat, Jr.
Nassau County Poet Laureate

IN GRATITUDE

NASSAU COUNTY POET LAUREATE COMMITTEE
Paula Camacho, Coordinator; Beverly Kotch, Outreach Chairperson; Maria Manobianco, Public Relations Director; Ursula Nouza, Outreach; and a special thank you to Judy Turek, Chairperson of the School Poetry Project for her work and dedication which made this project possible.

Consultants
Susan Astor, Poet-in-the-Schools and Sue Korman, Grant Assistant

FREEPORT MEMORIAL LIBRARY
For their support and sponsorship of this project with a special thank you for all their help to Maggie Marino, Coordinator of Adult Services
and Maryellen Cantanno, Youth Services Librarian.

NASSAU GRANTS FOR THE ARTS
This project is made possible, in part, with public funds from the New York State Council on the Arts' Decentralization Program, administered by the Long Island Arts Council at Freeport.

SPECIAL FRIENDS
There are people who give their time and talent from the kindness of their heart.

Thank you to Mankh (Walter E. Harris III) for his patience and assistance in working diligently with the committee on all the necessary details to produce this amazing anthology.

Thank you to Joan Marg for her "behind the scenes" generous assistance in those unexpected aspects that required extra help in the production of this book.

For their encouragement and support to their students, thank you to all school personnel for proving that *poetry lives in Nassau County!*

To all the Journal Sponsors, thank you for helping us make dreams come true.

TABLE OF CONTENTS

KINDERGARTEN

KINDERGARTEN GOLD MEDAL AWARD

Thomas Boland
Homestead School, Garden City, NY

My name is Tommy
I love to play with toys
My brothers are Brian and Bo
We're the "Boland Boys"
But wait there's one more
My big sister Katie
I can't forget her
She is a lady.

~ ~ ~

KINDERGARTEN SILVER MEDAL AWARD

Frank Santeramo
Homestead School, Garden City, NY

I lost my first tooth in school
I was excited as you can see.
Then I really lost my tooth
I still wonder where it could be.

~ ~ ~

KINDERGARTEN BRONZE MEDAL AWARD

Juliette Pinkiert
Oceanside Kindergarten Center #6, Oceanside, NY

Grandpa's Rehab

My grandpa is meeting a few friends,
He eats wonderful food,
He has a nice bed to sleep in
But, it is boring for me!

KINDERGARTEN HONORABLE MENTIONS
In alphabetic order by author

Kelly Brennan
Homestead School, Garden City, NY

Winter

In winter it snows
Animals hibernate
Singing in the winter show
Sledding down big hills
Drinking hot cocoa

~ ~ ~

James Burke
Homestead School, Garden City, NY

My name is James
I'm five years old
I have twin sisters who are two
So my mom and dad struck gold.

~ ~ ~

Natalie DiFusco
Oceanside Kindergarten Center #6, Oceanside, NY

My Cat

I love him
Playing a lot
Eating food
Catching feathers
Sleeping in his bed
Purring, purring
He's the best!

Sarah Fetherston
Homestead School, Garden City, NY

Winter

Beautiful winter trees
White snow covered grass
Making snowmen with a carrot for his nose
Putting on cozy jackets
Opening presents Christmas morning

~ ~ ~

Jessica Hoffman
Oceanside Kindergarten Center #6, Oceanside, NY

Thanksgiving

Watching the parade on TV
Getting ready to go to Grandma Sheila's house
Playing with cousins
Turkey
A fun Day

~ ~ ~

Brendan McGovern
Homestead School, Garden City, NY

Winter

Snowball fights
Presents to open
Snowmen to decorate
Wreaths on doors
Santa and Rudolf on the roof

Olivia Mitchell
Oceanside Kindergarten Center #6, Oceanside, NY

Naomi

My sister
Playing soccer
Going to the park
Reading books
Lots of fun
My sister!

~ ~ ~

Kelly O'Neill
Homestead School, Garden City, NY

Winter

Me and Kevin making snow angels
Cold weather
Bundle up to go outside
Playing in the snow
Snuggly pajamas

~ ~ ~

Emma Romano
Oceanside Kindergarten Center #6, Oceanside, NY

Fall

I see leaves falling down
The trees are very bare
I hear the wind blowing
Blowing through my ears
I feel cold and then I know
Fall is very near

Mark Satler
Oceanside Kindergarten Center #6, Oceanside, NY

Turtles

Hard shell
Sharp claws
Walks on little feet
Little hands for eating
Turtles sleep in the ocean

~ ~ ~

Luke Strianese
Oceanside Kindergarten Center #6, Oceanside, NY

Dogs

Dogs love me
And dogs love you
When they're happy
They kiss you!

~ ~ ~

Riley Weinstein
Oceanside Kindergarten Center #6, Oceanside, NY

Snowman Snowman

Roll a big ball
Add 2 more balls.
Then put a carrot
Then put a mouth
3 big buttons going down
That's all!

1ST GRADE

Elana Pocress
Walter S. Boardman Elementary School #9, Oceanside, NY

Wonderful School

I can see
Hexagonal cozy corner
Pink flowers

I can taste
Saucy pizza
Stretchy mozzarella sticks

I can hear
Lockers slamming
Footsteps walking

I can smell
Tasty chicken nuggets
Fresh air

I can touch
Hard notebooks
Pointy pencils

What a wonderful
School I'm in

Mahika Gupta
Lee Avenue School, Hicksville, NY

Music

Music is what makes you move
Music is what makes you groove
Music can be good or bad depending on how it's used
Music can make you choose different clothes to wear
Music can make you change your hair
Music can make you choose new friends
Music can make you want to dance
Music can make you fight
Music can make everything all right
Music can take care of you when you're alone
Music can make everything feel like home
Music can harm and take away
Music can make you want to stay
Music is the only friend I have
Music is my mom and dad
Music is what keeps me alive
Music is when I feel like I can't survive

1ST GRADE BRONZE MEDAL AWARD

Rachel Ronan
South Oceanside Road Elementary School #4, Oceanside, NY

The Turkey Strut

See all the little turkeys up in a tree,
All the little turkeys like to hide from me.
Please stand still don't make a sound,
You'll see the turkeys as they strut around.
All the little turkeys go wobble, wobble, wobble,
All the little turkeys just like this.
All the little turkeys go gobble, gobble, gobble,
All the little turkeys just like this!

1ST GRADE HONORABLE MENTIONS
In alphabetic order by author

Fitzgerald Alcindor
Meadow Elementary School, Baldwin, NY

Don't cry

Don't cry
Please don't cry
Shy little guy

~ ~ ~

Zoe Allain
Oaks Elementary School #3, Oceanside, NY

Winter is my favorite
Season
Listen here,
I'll tell the
Reason
I drink hot cocoa
Very slow
And sit and watch
The white white snow.

Jamie Behar
Fulton Avenue Elementary School #8, Oceanside, NY

Green

Green as fireworks shooting in the sky.
Green as a frog hopping everywhere.
Green as a turtle swimming in the pond.
Green as the grass tickling my skin.
Green as a garden growing plants.
Green as a candle in the menorah.
Green as a valley with bushes so pretty.
Green as the mittens I wear.
Green as a butterfly flying so high.
Green as a scarf that I wear.
Green as the leaf falling down.
Green as the tree so big.
Green as the bug in the nighttime.

~ ~ ~

K.C. Carlson
North Oceanside Road Elementary School #5, Oceanside, NY

Ice Fishing

Ice
Fishing
With my dad.
Puffy camouflage jackets
Sitting on benches.
Poles stabbing into ice and snow.
Picks crack open the ice
Special gloves reach
to catch
the bait.

Emma Cohen
Fulton Avenue Elementary School #8, Oceanside, NY

What is Colors

What is pink
Pink is a flamingo pink as it is

What is blue
Blue is a blue robin singing in the wind up in a tree

What is black
Black is a penguin waddling away to the nearest pool

What is red
Red is a ladybug crawling away in the grass

What is yellow
Yellow sun up to God and the moon

~ ~ ~

Mia Antonette Dircks
Central Boulevard Elementary School, Bethpage, NY

The Moon

The moon shines in the dark.
Also the sun shines in the dark.
All the stars are in the sky
lighting up the world.
It looks so pretty!

Catherine Henn
Walter S. Boardman Elementary School #9, Oceanside, NY

Pumpkin

Spins
Like   a   dreidel.
Small,   heavy,   hard.
Orange   like   the   sun.
Curvey,   brown,   skinny stem.
Round   as   a   ball.
Funny   little   Jack-o-lantern.

~ ~ ~

Michael Jager
South Oceanside Road Elementary School #4, Oceanside, NY

School

To Gym we go
To Gym we go
Hay ho the derio
They came to learn that day
To Art we go
To Art we go
Hay ho the derio
They came to learn that day
To school we go
To school we go
Hay ho the derio
They all came to learn that day

Anna Malin
Florence A. Smith Elementary School #2, Oceanside, NY

Mary

I know a girl named Mary.
She was a magical fairy.
She had a pet rat.
That she turned into a hat.
She was tired and she sat.
Then fell asleep on the mat.

~ ~ ~

Emma Nastro
Oaks Elementary School #3, Oceanside, NY

Wondrous sights
Ice skating
Nice jingle bells
Toys
Emma's birthday
Rainbows

Dale Revelant
Oaks Elementary School #3, Oceanside, NY

Colors

Purple can be
A flower
A shirt
A paper
A grape

Blue can be
A bluebird
A pond
A batch of blueberries
A lot of sky
        Colors are fun.

~ ~ ~

Mary Reynolds
Florence A. Smith Elementary School #2, Oceanside, NY

Black Cat

I saw a black cat
With a big hat.
He was cooking with a big pot
Next to a small cot.
He was cooking over a big pit
With a small cooking kit.

2ND GRADE

Christina Korotki
Walter S. Boardman Elementary School #9, Oceanside, NY

The Cold

When it's cold
I cuddle
Near my fireplace
Get next to it
It's warm
It sounds like
Rice crispies crackling
I cuddle
Near my mom
But
The fire is not
As warm
As her hugs.

2ND GRADE SILVER MEDAL AWARD

Brendan Feehan
North Oceanside Road Elementary School #5, Oceanside, NY

Stapler

The stapler
Bites its prey
like a cobra.

Grace Anne McKenna
Wantagh Elementary School, Wantagh, NY

Seasons

Winter

The color of Winter is white. It is the first season. In the Winter we go ice skating. We play in the snow and have snowball fights. We drink hot cocoa. Wow! We go sleigh riding and go bump, bump down the hill. Wow! The trees are bare and the snow is melting. Winter is changing into Spring.

Spring

Spring is colorful. When I close my eyes I see pink, green, and white. The Easter Bunny comes with goodies and toys. The trees grow buds and leaves. Spring is healing from Winter. The plants grow back. Wow! The vegetables and fruits are coming back. Wow! The sun is warming my face and the fresh air feels refreshing to breathe.

Summer

Wow! Hot Summer days! I see the color red. At the beach we swim in the ocean, build sandcastles, and watch the boats go by. We swim in the pool and play games at camp. Thunder booms and lightning flashes. Skies are grey and rain comes falling down. Wow! I see a rainbow. It is red, orange, yellow, green, blue, and purple.

Fall

In the Fall, the leaves are changing to red, orange, yellow, and green. Wow! Aren't the leaves a mess? Let's rake them. We jump and play in the leaf piles. We go trick-or-treating, see scarecrows, and carve jack-o-lanterns. We pick red, yellow, and green apples at the orchard. We go to a pumpkin farm and pick pumpkins from the fields. Wow! Wasn't that a great year!

Kristen Babel
Fulton Avenue Elementary School #8, Oceanside, NY

My Feelings

When it's rainy
I'm glum

When it's sunny
I'm happy

When it's foggy
I'm sleepy

When it's windy
I'm torn apart.

Connor Calkin
South Oceanside Road Elementary School #4, Oceanside, NY

My Dog

Sammy is my dog.
She's a lab and she's all black.
She gets the ball and brings it back.
She bites my cat.
Imagine that.
My dog runs down the stairs.
She runs so quick it makes big flares.
She runs back
And gives my cat a heart attack.
In my cat's dreams he freezes
In a breeze
And he has big knees.
My dog listens to anyone good.
She even eats her broccoli when she should.
She listens to my dad
And never acts bad.
I am glad
She is not bad.

Clyde Chisolm
Fulton Elementary School, Hempstead, NY

A Poem about Santa

The Christmas tree has a lot of lights.
I gave it to Santa and he was nice.
I put out the fire in the chimney so he can go up higher.
I was near the Christmas tree and Santa fell on me.
I cried and Santa tried to say good-bye.
I opened my present and it was a book bag.
Santa wiped my tears with a dirty rag.
I played and Santa prayed.
I watered the plants and Santa did a dance.
I made a building and Santa made millions.
I had a pig and Santa put on my mother's wig.
Santa had to look very hard to get away from my St. Bernard
because he was too afraid to go in my backyard.
The Christmas tree had a lot of lights.
I gave it to Santa and he was very nice.

~ ~ ~

Brooke Cody
Bayville Primary School, Bayville, NY

Trees in Autumn

The trees bend
The wind blows
Leaves are pulled off the branches
Bald trees stand like statues
Feeling cold without their
colorful coats.

Justin Darvick
North Oceanside Road Elementary School #5, Oceanside, NY

The Mirror

The mirror
is a universe
that you
and I
cannot go into
and
the words
are spelled backwards.

~ ~ ~

Noah Eisel
Fulton Avenue Elementary School #8, Oceanside, NY

The Snowfall

Clouds opening and letting go
snow
F
  A
    L
      L
       I
        N
          G from the sky

laying cold blankets
over the earth
crunched up
pieces of glass
exploding on the ground.

Molly Eisenberg
Fulton Avenue Elementary School #8, Oceanside, NY

Angels

Sweet
floating
little angels
fly in the sky

creating friendship
around the world
making us friends
until the end

then we'll become the ones---
the angels
that never die

~ ~ ~

Beatriz Flores-Valle
Fulton Elementary School, Hempstead, NY

At Christmas

At Christmas
I will see
a polar bear calling me.

He will tell me to write a note
for him to his friend
Mr. Fox, so he can be happy.

When I am done he will give me a
polar bear hug.

Irene Kavadias
South Oceanside Road Elementary School #4, Oceanside, NY

Deep Inside A Poem

When a poem is near it…
hits me like a rock.
When poetry flows by me it
is like wind going back and
forth

It bounces me up then puts me
back on the ground

Poems inspire my feelings
it bursts me out and flows into my pencil
it is amazing how…
unique it is.

~ ~ ~

Randy Lorenzo
North Oceanside Road Elementary School #5, Oceanside, NY

The Stapler

One touch
teeth biting
its food of paper.
It opens its mouth.
Its tooth fell out.

Anthony Madsen
Bayville Primary School, Bayville, NY

Building a Snowman

I built a snowman
He's getting smaller and smaller
and he melted
the only thing left

was snow all around me
so I went inside
really, really sad.

I wonder how he feels now,
all alone on the ground.

~ ~ ~

Madison White
Lenox School, Baldwin, NY

Winter Time

In winter time I taste hot,
burning hot chocolate
on the tip of my tongue.

In winter time I feel
my numb fingertips
and the wind
blowing beside
me.

In winter time
I hear freezing,
chattering teeth.

3RD GRADE

Jillian Duryea
North Oceanside Road Elementary School #5, Oceanside, NY

The Big War

Her words slapped me across the face
Getting angrier every second
Starting to get like a Royal Rumble
Starting to do the same thing as her
It was chaos
Our friends holding us down
Building like a war
Soon it was all over
No one won
It was all over
The chaos
The words
The war
The Royal Rumble
Everything
Including our friendship
Those words were strong
Never would they be said again

Logan Freedman
A.P. Willits School, Syosset, NY

Baseball Fever

It was a dry heated mid summer day
And the players were ready to play
The pitcher threw the pitch straight down the pipe
The batter got set and took a glorious swipe
He hit the ball way over the fence
The pitcher shook his head it made no sense
He felt the pressure standing on the mound
He let an important run in, his heart began to pound
He squeezed the ball before he released
He smoked three in a row and the inning ceased
The next inning came the other team was up
They needed some hits so they could catch up
They weren't that good so they had lots of trouble
But then the time came where they hit a double
The team was tired, they were running out of steam
The coach screamed words about getting tough and mean
The sweat of the underdog soaked their uniform
We needed a streak, a bit of luck and thunderous storm
The next three batters cracked weak bouncing singles, the team started to jam
Big Billy was up; strike one, strike two, then a grand slam
One score needed to win, the man made it to first
The next man came to the plate and tasted the game and felt the thirst
The next batter came up to try to drive him in
He had no success so they failed to win
Both teams went home with their heads up high
As they went different ways, they said their goodbyes
It was a great day to play
It was a mid summer day

3RD GRADE BRONZE MEDAL AWARD

Halle Gumpel
Meadow Drive Elementary School, Albertson, NY

When I'm sad,
I feel like a piano
With dust all over my keys, no one
playing them.

I cannot hear anything
As if my strings are broken,
I feel very lonely
in the silence of the room.

Chelsea Buda
Fulton Avenue Elementary School #8, Oceanside, NY

My Grandpa

My grandpa was grateful and nice

He passed away
I'll never forget that sad day

He would tell me stories that were true
And about the things he used to do

I love him so,
My heart won't ever let him go

He was in the war
But not anymore

This happened when I was little
He would also tell me riddles

I used to call him "Pa, Sid"

When I think of him
I feel his eyes looking in my heart
Saying, "I love you"
Then I would say back, "I love you, too"
Even if you are in heaven
I love you Pa, Sid.

Nicholas Ciminelli
Meadow Drive Elementary School, Albertson, NY

Frogs sing rainforest songs
hopping and humming to the beat
the rivers rushing
and the logs rolling
the frogs hopping in the chorus.

~ ~ ~

Naya Ghirdarry
North Oceanside Road Elementary School #5, Oceanside, NY

Grandma's House

I like the taste of turkey
Any time throughout the year
But it never seems to taste as good
As when Thanksgiving is here.

Could be it's all the sweets
That are cooked with it to eat
But I think it's eating at Grandma's house
That makes it such a treat!

~ ~ ~

Julia Kelly
Meadow Drive Elementary School, Albertson, NY

When I'm lonely I feel like a teddy bear
unstuffed and ragged
left on your bed
no one beside me.
I have tears going through
my big black button eyes
hoping that someone will pick me up.

Sophia Levenson
A.P. Willits School, Syosset, NY

Snapping Alligators

Alligator Alligator six feet long
Mouth so big and teeth so strong

You look at me with your eyes open wide
You may not know I'm just taking a ride

Over the saw grass and lily pads we flow
The plants and animals we see as we go

Alligators, frogs, snails and birds too
There is so much to see and a real lot to do

I am off to see the alligators if you don't mind
Come along with me and let's see what we find

~ ~ ~

Angela Mayo
Fulton Avenue Elementary School #8, Oceanside, NY

The Talking Crayon

A crayon in a box all snug and tight,
A crayon in a box with no light,
Pushing and shoving all through the night,
I can't take this anymore said little red,
If we stay here any longer we'll lose all our lead,
On the count of 3 we'll all break free,
1...2...3 GO!
POP goes the box,
All crayons run out,
Wow that was a close one,
I'm glad that we're out,
Out the door and down the stairs out the front door
Wow that was a close one I'm glad we're out!

Alighnte McCormick
John Street School, Franklin Square, NY

Winter Rock Band

Winter fun is here
I make a snowman rock band
They play till they melt.

~ ~ ~

Brendan McFall
North Oceanside Road Elementary School #5, Oceanside, NY

The Hit of My Dreams

First time up at bat
Waiting
Hearing nothing
Waiting for a pitch
A good pitch
Nothing comes
Nothing comes
Showing off
Bat waving
Tap the plate
Still no pitch
Wait some more
Pitch!
Foul ball!
Waiting
Wanting another
Another pitch
It comes in
Bang!
Bat meets ball
Ball soaring
Fast, furious
I hustle
Faster, faster!
Breathing fast as ever
Rounding first base
Now second, third

> >

Home Run!
Huff, Puff
Trying to catch a breath
Curtain call
Home Run
Feeling like a pro
Never forgetting
That day,
That hit
That experience
The hit of my dreams
Floating away
Chugging water
Sitting like a statue on the bench
More people watching
Our team winning
So happy as if we just won The World Series

~ ~ ~

Jake Mullin
South Grove Elementary School, Syosset, NY

Rain, Turn to Snow

I woke up on Christmas morning
To find warm rain falling
Drip, drop, drip, drop,
I sat and thought about
How that rain should be snow
Christmas was incomplete
I had the presents, the family
But something was missing
I waited for a long, long time
With my new iPod on my lap
I waited until one o'clock
By that time I had given up
Until I looked outside
Cold, white snow was falling
I slipped on my coat, boots and mittens
And then I ran outside

Abel Ninan
North Oceanside Road Elementary School #5, Oceanside, NY

Walking

Walking
With
My
Dad
In
The
Blizzard
The cold wind roaring past
My whole body quivering
I close my eyes
As the strong wind sails against me
Those winds
Stronger than a tornado
Those winds
Making my lips shut close
I huddle
Together
With my dad
As
The
Strongest
Winds swish
Fiercefully by
Back and forth
Back and forth
As
My dad
And
I
Hold on tight.

Sebastian Posillico
Meadow Drive Elementary School, Albertson, NY

Little Elf Friends

We are like two mischievous elves
running around getting in and out of trouble.
Nobody knows what we're going to do next.
But if you need us, look for the little hats.

~ ~ ~

Julia Ruskin
John Philip Sousa Elementary School, Port Washington, NY

A Candy Shop Limerick

My mom took me to the candy shop.
I bought a little lollipop
Red, green, blue, yellow,
The colors looked ever so mellow,
Swirled on my lollipop.

4TH GRADE

4TH GRADE GOLD MEDAL AWARD

Chava Dimaio
South Oceanside Road Elementary School #4, Oceanside, NY

Volcano Of Stuff!!

In my desk there is a book
There's also a test I once took
An ant that is smashed on the top of my folder
A warm, squishy ice pack which has to get colder
A toy tiger which formed thirty six eyes
And deep in my desk are some leftover fries
A sharpener which looks like a racer
And one picture of me hugging a glacier
A miniature dog on a miniature bed
And somewhere in there I think a fly is dead
A glue bottle which lost its cap
And on my notebook is some sticky tree sap
A Kooky Pen which lost its ink
And some crumpled old postcards which are pink
Some icky green slugs which are really slow
But hey where did my pencil go?

4TH GRADE SILVER MEDAL AWARD

Ashley Polsinelli
John Street School, Franklin Square, NY

In the Woods

Walking home through the woods,
I saw my old dog Brandy.
She died two years ago,
But I saw her.

She was trying to tell me something-
Then she disappeared.
I heard a cry-
So I followed, until I came upon my brother.

I asked him what was wrong
"I saw."
"Saw what?" I said. – The Dead.

We started home.
I thought about what he said.
Then Brandy, my dog came to my head.

As I walked in the door,
"Oh." My mom said.
"Would you like something to eat?"
She spoke with dread.

My mom made me soup,
Putting one bowl on the table.
Then I thought.

Why was it him not me.
Why did my brother have to go?
In that accident three years ago?
Not me, not me.
Why could it not have been me?

He was only three years old,
Now he's gone forever.
Only to be seen on my walks.

Hannah Zwick
South Grove Elementary School, Syosset, NY

Nightmares

Tossing, turning, moaning, groaning
in my sleep.
Nightmares pitch black like a pool of tar.
The trees' shadows
grabbing,
scratching,
lurking,
and
spying
like monsters.
Owls screeching, piercing my ears.
Thump, then another, then another, like a
heartbeat.
The heartbeats turn into a stampede of
creatures, all shapes and sizes
coming at me.
I scream!!!!
I sit up in bed.
Everything's gone.
I try to go back to sleep.
It's not easy, but I do.
Hoping another nightmare doesn't come
creeping through.

Vincent Basso
Rushmore Avenue Elementary School, Carle Place, NY

Imagine

Imagine you were on a bird
flying on its wing.
Imagine you saved the world
with only just a string.
Imagine you sang a song
that broke everyone's heart.
Imagine you built a robot
that took everything apart.
Imagine you were on a boat
set sail at sea.
Imagine you were in a peaceful place
as peaceful as can be.

~ ~ ~

Ruthie Bergman
Winthrop Avenue School, Bellmore, NY

Autobiographical Poem

Who is a kind and playful girl.
Who needs water and care.
Who wants a Wii and longer hair.
Who feels happy when playing baseball, sad when in trouble.
Who wishes for her sisters to stop annoying her on the double.
Who is loved by her family and friends.
Who gives love and affection until the end.
Who lives in Bellmore, 11710, New York, USA, North America, Planet Earth,
Milky Way Galaxy.

Valeria Caamano
North Oceanside Road Elementary School #5, Oceanside, NY

Rose

As soft as a pillow,
As red as a ripe, red cherry,
As green as well-watered grass,
And as beautiful as my mom.

With the help of the wind
the rose dances.
With the help of the water
the rose matures and
comes out to say, "Hello!"
The sun makes her glow.
Her arms are like the shoulders of a dress
and
she starts to dance.

I want to be like the rose.
I want to be red and green and beautiful too.
I want to mature with the water.
I want to dance with the wind,
And I want to come out to say, "Hello!"
I want to be like the rose.

Serina Cafiero
Florence A. Smith Elementary School #2, Oceanside, NY

What I Think About Fall

Fall sounds like cats meowing in my yard
as they look for a cozy place to sleep.
Fall sounds like kids stepping in candy wrappers
as they dive into piles of leaves.

Fall tastes like crunchy candy in my mouth
like they are having a party.
Fall tastes like yummy, sweet vanilla cake
going down my throat like it is going on a field trip.

Fall smells like tasty turkey baking in the oven
like it's getting a suntan.
Fall smells like bubbling hot chocolate cooling off
so it is not too hot for me to drink.

Fall looks like kids trading all of their candy
so they can get even better candy.
Fall looks like hundreds of kids in scary costumes
racing from door to door begging for candy.

Fall feels like cold wind punching me
like I was fighting it.
Fall feels like jumping in the rough, colorful leaves
and getting buried by them.

Lorelei Calboreanu
North Oceanside Road Elementary School #5, Oceanside, NY

Sparkling Fish

Splish
Splash
Twinkling like a shooting star
Swimming fast like a plane
Splish
Splash
Diving up and down
In the
Beautiful blue ocean
Splish
Splash
Swimming away
From the
Great
White
Shark
Moving gracefully through the water
Colors of orange and gold
Swimming faster
Than ever
Almost
There
Silence
No fish
Just blood
In the
Blue sea
The fish is gone
So sad
Little bit guilty
Gone forever
In the
Great
White
Sharks
Belly
Gone forever
Bye
Sparkling fish

Alexis Chiofalo
North Oceanside Road Elementary School #5, Oceanside, NY

A Wet Scary Monster

A scary monster
All wet
You can run away from it
When he gets
Mad
He will
Stand
Big and tall
Trying to
Scare you
He will push you to the
Hard,
Wet,
Rough sand
When he is near the yellow sun and the blue sky
He begins to melt
He becomes smaller
Until he is so small
He is now only a small ripple
Around your ankle
Look out at the blue dark open sea
The scary monster
Is coming back
To start all over again
Will it get you?

Annette Gutnik
Norman J. Levy-Lakeside School, Merrick, NY

The Lonely Room
      after Van Gogh's "Bedroom in Arles"

Nobody comes in.
Door shut, window half open.
Nobody comes in.
Bed all ready for sleep
but nobody comes in.
Picture crooked on the wall
but nobody comes in.
Picture of person in the room
feeling happy, but it is only a picture.
Nobody comes in.

~ ~ ~

Adrienne Kolanovic
Maria Regina School, Seaford, NY

Purple

Purple reminds me of
the night sky while it is raining.
My winter jacket
Barney
Kings and queens in their velvet robes of purple
My mom's cell phone
Lent and Easter
Lavender
Violets
Heather
My shirt
The mountain range in Croatia
My doll's shiny hair.

Caroline Longo
North Oceanside Road Elementary School #5, Oceanside, NY

Winter Freeze

The fall closes the deal and shakes hands with the wind,
winter is officially here.
Winter starts by the lake
moving the ice like soldiers
across the body of water it curls then,
splash!
It freezes.
Then he moves to the trees
and coils them in a blanket of snow.
He scatters ice crystals about.
Magic begins
in the bitter brisk.
Snow starts to fall,
trees sing,
and the snowflakes dance
to the beautiful music of tip, tap, tapping
as it sways to the ground,
rings in your ear
and you say,
"Winter is officially here!"
As the snow falls to the ground
it moves across the grass
it freezes,
it freezes,
it freezes.
Winter is officially here.
Winter goes back to his kingdom
and thinks to himself,
"My snow is a butterfly"
and he settles down to sleep.

Sara Murphy
North Oceanside Road Elementary School #5, Oceanside, NY

The Dancing Push

Carnations need water
Like babies need care
Like I need dance
Without it I feel
Like a car without gas
Swoosh! Swoosh! Go my feet
Slowly, the beat takes me away
To another land
Where dance is dear
Where dance is a need
Where dance dazzles
No need for diaries when you're a dancer
Feelings are expressed without words
Without dance my world would be dull
My life is that of a dancer's
Twirling, tapping in the dark sky
My heart beats as fast as a cheetah
My shoes become best friends with the stage
When I sway across it on my toes
The audience cheers, whistles and dances along in excitement
The lights shine their sun-like rays on ME!
Butterflies roam around in my stomach
As I sway across the stage again
I feel a push
The dancing push

~ ~ ~

Paul Schell
North Oceanside Road Elementary School #5, Oceanside, NY

The Lizard

The lizard is a timid thing
That cannot dance or fly or sing;
He hunts for bugs beneath the floor
And longs to be a dinosaur

William Vandewater
North Oceanside Road Elementary School #5, Oceanside, NY

The Mountain Of Fur

```
                T
            N       A
            U       I
            O       N
   The      M       of    fur
```
as soft as a blanket
pounces off like a jackrabbit
Swish!
Crackle!
The sound of food makes her dash
as fast as superman.
She gobbles the food down
like a stapler chewing its paper prey
and the food disappears.
She zooms straight to her toys,
like a cheetah in the jungle.
She looks all the way up
toys out of reach
and gets a good grip …
BOOM!
In a lickety split
she is trotting
all over her toys.
At night she is back
```
                T
            N       A
            U       I
            O       N
  As the    M          of fur at the end
```
of my bed.
My cat Oreo.

5TH GRADE

5TH GRADE GOLD MEDAL AWARD

Courtney Capobianco
Florence A. Smith Elementary School #2, Oceanside, NY

Don't go

Crashing
Crashing
Crashing
Cars flashing lights on TV
People running people screaming
Then we get the call
He's hurt
He's hurt
He's hurt
I said don't go
My heart was beating as fast as a cheetah
Next morning he's dead
Tears coming out like waterfalls
I go to my nana's house every September 11,
We get
Flowers
Flowers
Flowers
As colorful as a rainbow
We put them up on a pole
I say I'll "Never Forget"

Amanda Andersen
North Oceanside Road Elementary School #5, Oceanside, NY

I am a Pencil

I am a pencil.
I wear a pink hat.
There's not much to say,
I'm as simple as that.

I am a pencil.
I lay in the desk.
For when I am tired,
That is where I rest.

I am a pencil.
I dance on the page.
With all the eraser shavings,
It's like my very own parade.

I am a pencil.
I like to write,
But I'm afraid my sharp point might break.
So, I'll be extra careful,
Just for the writer's sake.

Lindsay Hass
A.P. Willits School, Syosset, NY

The Images of Hanukah

It is Hanukah.

I see the lights on the menorah.
    Each one glimmering.
        Standing for the eight days of Hanukah.

I hear the Hebrew prayer so important.

Dreidels are dancing across the floor.
    Everyone hopes for the prize…
        of the chocolate coins!

I smell the sweet and appetizing latkes
    with applesauce for dipping.

I see people dancing the hora,
    And singing Hebrew prayers.

I see the Star of David in the window
    and on every girl's neck.

I hear kids listening to the story of Hanukah
    And other old tales.

I see men and boys wearing their yarmulkes.

And I now know it is Hanukah!

Ashley Anglade
Cedarhurst Number 5 School, Cedarhurst, NY

Snow Ice and Wind

Snow is
The soft
White blanket
I sleep
With
Snow is
The paper
I write on
That makes
My
Picture
Ice is
The place
Where
I will
Skate
Ice is
The heart
That sits in
A selfish
Person
Wind is
My serenity
That keeps
Me calm
Wind is
The peace
That flows
In my soul

Suleyma Arroyo
Fulton Elementary School, Hempstead, NY

When I Was Little...

When I was little my mom used to pinch my cheeks
Now she bites them

When I was little my dad used to carry me
Now I'm too heavy

When I was little I used to say silly words
Now I speak in sentences

When I was little I didn't understand teachers
Now I understand almost everything they teach

When I was little I had short hair
Now I have nice, long red hair

When I was little I slept in a crib
Now I sleep in a bigger bed

When I was little my mom used to brush my two bottom teeth
Now I brush all 32 of them myself

When I was little I used to kiss my mom
Now I kiss her belly because she has twins inside

Brianna Bonagura
Seaford Manor School, Seaford, NY

A Trip to the Beach

I walk by the salt water so cold,
But it feels good after going on the long path of hot sand,
I look at the gray minnows that watch my every move,
I run along the edge of the water letting the breeze push me,
Looking down I see all the pretty shells,
Then there was a little object moving,
I look closer at it and I see a hermit crab with a pretty swirled shell,
I put it in my blue bucket,
Then I get called for lunch,
I eat my favorite sandwich, peanut butter and jelly,
Then I let the hermit crab go,
Afterwards at home I can still smell the sea water in my hair.

~ ~ ~

Ruthie Gottesman
Solomon Schechter Day School of Nassau County, Jericho, NY

The Black Night

The black night
Swallowed into darkness
I'm mixed in

I take another step
And enter my cozy bed
It makes me feel warm

I look out my window
And see the starry night
And the bright moon
I feel like I'm flying

Then I close my eyes
Feeling nothing but stillness
The next thing I hear
The chirping of the morning!

Philip Ko
A.P. Willits School, Syosset, NY

Winter Mornings

One winter morning, I smelled fresh hot chocolate waiting for me ...
    ... at the kitchen table,
        ... waiting for me to drink it.

It tasted thick and creamy.
    When I drank it ...
        I felt all warm inside ...

When I looked out the kitchen window ...
    I saw the nice, white crispy snow
        ... that had fallen while I was asleep.

So I went outside ...
    to make a snowman ...
        that would make my brother smile like ...
            he had never smiled before.

Outside, I touch the crispy snow and start to pack it.
    I roll the packed snow to make big snowballs.
        Next, I stack the balls on top of each other.
        The snowman is complete.

I then remember my brother last time ... Crying!
    because he couldn't make a snowman
        because the snow had melted.

I see my brother come outside ...
    But he is crying.
        Why?

He wanted to make the snowman with me ...
So together we make another big snowman ... next to the first one.
    And then ...   My brother smiled like he never smiled before.

Emily Mendelson
Barnum Woods School, East Meadow, NY

Mealworms,
Cool creatures,
Hiding under leaves,
Very worried running from us,
Adult.

Mealworms,
Thigmotactic,
Press against the wall they're on,
Excited when we play with them,
Larva.

Mealworms,
Always active
Walk as fast as they can,
Like to live in the warm weather,
Insects.

Mealworms,
Are really fun,
Molts exoskeleton,
First egg, larva, pupa, adult,
Little.

Mealworms,
Astonishing,
Cannot see very well,
Tickle with a soft pipe-cleaner
Don't care.

Mealworms,
Different colors,
Do not drink anything,
Are very small like a crayon,
Mealworms.

Brianne Polehinke
George H. McVey Elementary School, East Meadow, NY

My Wonderful Mother

You are the candle of hope
That guides me through everything
Difficult.
Your eyes shine like diamonds,
Your smile's like sunshine
On a cloudy day.
You comfort me,
You understand me,
When something's wrong.
Mom,
This is your day
Enjoy it,
Cherish it,
Make it a memory.

Juliet L. Rafanelli
Bowling Green Elementary School, Westbury, NY

Strong, Fierce WIND

WHERE AM I GOING?

I smell leaves
while I'm being
blown away to
a dirty, dark place
ALONE

I hear the colorful
leaves crunching
on the sidewalk
by large feet

WHERE AM I GOING?

I see nothing
at all for this is
my dream

WHERE AM I GOING?

For what is ahead
I can't foresee because
this is a dream, the
best one I've
ever had

Tamara Saxman
Mattlin Middle School, Plainview, NY

Things in the Night

The wind whispered my name, carrying the leaves
To drift towards the ground
As a leaf rustled, I could almost hear a witch's cackle
Ringing in my ears
Over and over again
Traveling through the night sky.

I could almost hear a goblin running after me
Bump! Thump! Bump!
Green as an avocado
Calling my name
I could hear the roar of a devil
The flapping wings of an angel
As I ran, and ran, and ran.

The witch cackled another mighty cackle
The goblin screeched a mighty screech
As I looked around
I saw goblins, ghosts, and wizards
All lining up for candy
"Trick or Treat!"
It was only Halloween.

Danielle Speziale
Cedarhurst Number 5 School, Cedarhurst, NY

Divorce

When they were arguing
My mommy sighed
I watched as my daddy
Started to cry
I looked at my brother
And pleaded with my eyes
It's okay he said
While a piece of me died

I felt the tear in my heart
Knowing that this
Was a new beginning for me
A new start as well for my family

That was the end
No more mommy and daddy
Together
No more whole family
The horrible thing
That threw my life a curveball
DIVORCE

Elizabeth Stiles
South Grove Elementary School, Syosset, NY

Conversing With the Wind

Swoosh!
I hear the wind race by outside.
I open the window to converse with the wind.
He is obviously at an anger state.
"Wind, what is wrong?"
He howls by without even answering.
I ask yet once more.
"Wind, what is wrong?"
Too angry to answer, I suppose!

Swoosh!
I feel the gentle wind kiss my face.
My feet clench to the sand.
I open my mouth to converse with the wind.
"Wind, how gentle you are!"
He slowly and in a subtle way sweeps my hair to my side.
Too calm and gentle to answer, I suppose!

Swoosh!
I feel the brisk and harsh wind freeze my bare nose.
I pull off my scarf to converse with the wind.
"Wind, how cold you are!"
No answer from his brisk strokes.
"Oh wind! Talk to me! Converse!"
The wind, in a bottomless, deep, understanding voice replies,
"Oh child, watch my actions. Actions, my little one, speak louder than words."

I ran around with a vast, blissful smile on my face.

Victoria Webb
William L. Buck School, Valley Stream, NY

Foxes
Nipping
Babies are born
Scampering in the snow
Cuddling in a comfy place
Arctic

6TH GRADE

Olivia Goldfarb
Great Neck North Middle School, Great Neck, NY

By Myself

When I'm by myself
And I close my eyes
I'm a stallion galloping through the meadow
I'm a bird soaring through the sky
I'm an ancient broken up jug from 10,000 B.C.
I'm a sad sad holocaust survivor
I'm the glorious Grand Canyon
I'm a famous explorer exploring America before we came
I'm a history project that deserves an A but got an F
I'm an orange paintbrush that cannot be put down
I'm a colorful rainbow right after it rains
I'm a bright light in the darkness
I'm an excited puppy when it first comes to its new home
I'm a tiger stalking its prey
I'm whatever I want to be
And when I open my eyes
What I care to be
Is me

Nicole Gemmiti
Garden City Middle School, Garden City, NY

The Shot Heard 'Round the World

April 19, 1775.
The night is cold, dark, unwelcoming.
British soldiers march onto the Lexington commons.
Left, right. Left, right.
Awakened are the angry American people.
On go their lamps, as they abandon their homes to confront the king's men.
Left, right. Left, right.
Across the snowy, damp city, their rant is heard by all.
The people are angry at the king for making America what it was.
Angry at taxes.
Angry at his soldiers.
Angry at Great Britain.
Foul words and snowballs are being thrust aimlessly
and without warning at the soldiers.
A soldier, confused, a sudden impulse has caused him to open fire.
He fires his gun and kills an American man.
It is silent.
It seems as if the shot was heard by all.
The shot heard 'round the world.
A historic shot.
The beginning of battle.
The beginning of war.
The beginning of revolution.
The beginning of history.

Michael Vincent Crapotta
Garden City Middle School, Garden City, NY

My Hush Puppy

You walk so close to the ground
Your stubby legs reveal you are a hound
The drooping, waving ears so long
With eyes so sad a look forlorn

Alert you are with your tail straight out
A welcomed signal for a hunting scout
When you detect a scent of fox ahead
You quickly dash to the river's edge

In days of ole the sight of a chase was thrilling
The pageantry of a foxhunt killing
You sound off with your howl so deep and loud
And the winner celebrates, for he is very proud

But here in the suburbs you are my sweet pet
Forever will I care for you, you must never fret
You have been named Flopsy because of your ears
Black, brown, and white, you are a sweet dear.

Monica Beeferman
Great Neck North Middle School, Great Neck, NY

Ashokan Memories

Going on the gorge hike
A beautiful stream was rushing by
There was a magnificent waterfall
And pretty rocks that formed the gorge
Hear slosh, slosh as you step in the mud
The steep deer trail was the challenge of the hike

Making apple cider was very fun
Turning the wheel to grind the apples,
Pressing them,
Seeing the juice flow out into the bucket
Delicious, hot apple cider warmed me up on the chilly day

Everyone canoeing was having a lot of fun
See the swimming ducks
Hear the waterfall in the background
And the crashing of metal when the canoes crashed
Feel the cold water as you get splashed

Traveling to the 1817 schoolhouse was very interesting
When walking in we curtseyed
Wearing the dunce cap,
Getting chased around the building,
Holding a wood log for raising your hand,
Writing with a quill,
And sitting on primers
It felt like we were actually in the year 1817

American Crossing was very inspiring
Learning many important lessons
Never give up,
Follow your dreams,
If you want something to happen, all you have to do is believe in yourself

Chloé Cristian
Great Neck North Middle School, Great Neck, NY

An Enchanting Dress

An alluring graceful dress behold
As light and ravishing as a single feather,
It was contented in a plastic cover
A dress so beautiful as a sunset in hot weather.

The silky architecture
Each stitch sewn in a magical way,
A golden lace top with a sun-colored sash
Would melt my heart away.

That puffy and fluffy skirt
So thick and silky sequined
A skirt that goes down 10 feet to the floor,
A fairy magical princess dress
The beauty of the shape galore.

A ravishing and lovely design
Of a Cinderella dress
Old and yellow
Lacy and mellow
Exciting as a quest,

My Nana's Wedding Dress.

Brian Darmstadt
Mineola Middle School, Mineola, NY

Death's Glory

The war begins as cannons blast
Dropping soldiers O so fast
Out on this battlefield
No one wins

As the intensity rises
Hazy smoke has men gasping for breath
As they plunge on into certain death
As they all fall
Death's chariot collects them all

As the cannons boom, men die
Sounds like thunder roaring O so high
As men fall,
Death's chariot collects them all.

Antonella Di Stefano
John Street School, Franklin Square, NY

I am

I am- a sister and a cousin of an Autistic child
I wonder- if they will ever find a cure
I hear- a voice calling "it will be okay"
I see- my reflection in the mirror
I want- my brother and my cousin to be normal
I am- a sister and a cousin of an Autistic child

I pretend- there is no such thing as Autism
I feel- John and Carlo's hands tapping on my shoulder
I touch- the world around me
I worry- my life will be horrible
I cry- when they embarrass me
I am- a sister and a cousin of an Autistic child

I understand- I should not be scared
I say- to myself "everything will be fine"
I dream- that it will go away
I try- to research and try to find a cure
I hope- they find a cure someday
I am- a sister and a cousin of an Autistic child

~ ~ ~

Emma P. Farrell
St. William the Abbot School, Seaford, NY

Lonely

When I'm lonely I feel like a pillow
wearing an ugly pillowcase.
No one sleeps on me and has dreams.
Even though I'm soft
nobody comes by me.

Hannah Courtney Isaac
Great Neck North Middle School, Great Neck, NY

White Canvas

My mind is as blank as a plain white canvas
It is ready to be painted on
But all deep thoughts
That I usually think
Seem to have vanished
Where is my inspiration?
It seems to have disappeared
Along with my thoughts
Now I feel hopeless
As if I am the only one in a field
During a harsh lightning storm
Where is my shelter?
Where are my friends?
I am lonelier than a single white rose
In a field full of purple lilies
So different than I
I need a savior
My knight in shining armor
But soon my fantasies slip away
Like when you're a child
Trying to drink clear water
Out of cupped hands
I know that eventually my thoughts will come back to me
For I need them to think of poetry
That will amaze the screaming crowds
Yet there is no reassurance
To comfort me like a soft, snuggly blanket
To erase my worries like an eraser erases one's penciled mistakes
S l o w l y
My barren mind is lifted
Through my head and out into a vast sea of dreams
Soft, cuddly, internally warming happy dreams
For without my worries
I am lighter than a feather,
And hold no resistance
To being pushed off into the clutches of sleep.

Samara Khan
Polk Street School, Franklin Square, NY

Veteran

You fought our country's battles,
You helped our country win.
You fought in wars that raged on,
And brought glory to your kin.

America adores you,
And with all that you've been through,
Oh, heroic veteran,
We really do thank you!

You've been through some hard times,
And lost people near and dear,
But you've done so much for our country,
It ought to be quite clear:

That you deserve the glory,
Of millions of hearts and minds,
That thank you for your services,
To America and mankind!

Veteran, we all will be
Sad when you are gone,
But even so, dear veteran,
Your legacy will live on!

Because of what you've done for us,
We will remember you.
All of the things you've done,
Most of us will never do!

Michael Kohen
John Street School, Franklin Square, NY

When Lee Surrendered To Grant

The blood was shed
The men were gone
The battlefields silent
The country in pieces
At the courthouse the armies stood
Brothers vs. Brothers
To think it took guns and cannons to fight
But it would end on paper
The war would end but it would take
Longer than that for our country to recover

~ ~ ~

Deepti Deepak Mahajan
Herricks Middle School, Albertson, NY

The Moon through the Telescope

As I look through a telescope the moon calls to me
A glowing crescent
Hiding its scars
Its wise solemn face made of rock
Staring blankly ahead
Its other side embalmed in darkness
Holding many mysteries
Its only companion the star
Shining with pride and happiness
Twinkling with joy at the moon
And as I close the lid of the telescope
I can see the last of the moon
Rolling sadly into the dark grey clouds
No longer wanting to be shown to the world
While it's merry companion stays behind
Smiling where the moon had been

Tara Pedian
Florence A. Smith Elementary School #2, Oceanside, NY

Mom

Knock, knock, knock
Slam, step, step, step
It must be my grandma here
To get us ready
But
In walks
My mother!
Gone for three months
Home
It was a horse
Stampeding through my body
Hugging and kissing all morning
As if school wasn't coming
Now
Life
Back to the way
It should be
Us
Together
again

Kathryn Romeo
North Oceanside Road Elementary School #5, Oceanside, NY

Life Without My GiGi

Life without GiGi seems hard and cold,
    She won't be here with me as I get old.
In the morning, when I get dressed,
    I sometimes think about her and I feel depressed.
When she got sick I prayed and prayed,
    The cancer in her body would go away.
I ask God, "Why did my GiGi die?"
    I get no answers and then I cry.
I loved my GiGi so much so,
    Life isn't the same since she had to go.
When GiGi died I was just about to turn eleven,
    I want her on earth, not in heaven!
Why did she have to leave? Why did she have to go?
    I loved her lots and I hope she had known.
I look at her photos of days gone by,
    I think about her life and I sometimes cry.
I miss GiGi's love and smile,
    Even when she was grumpy – it was just for a while.
I miss my great-grandmother so very much,
    I miss her face and her touch.
I remember at times her being a real tough cookie,
    But that was OK because I thought it was funny.
Life without GiGi may at times be rotten – BUT,
    My great-grandma "GiGi" will never be forgotten.

Eric Zeppa
Long Beach Middle School, Long Beach, NY

Pizza

I'm going to a restaurant
To eat my lunch today
The waitress says "What can I get ya"
I don't know what to say
I decide on some pizza, with pepperoni too
When I get my pizza
I chew and chew and chew
Then I get something yellow and red
I ask the waitress "What is that"
She says "This is pizza, you just ate the bread"

7TH GRADE

7TH GRADE GOLD MEDAL AWARD

Richard Feder
Great Neck North Middle School, Great Neck, NY

Birds and You

Have you ever felt the talons of a falcon
Or seen through an eagle's eye
Or maybe flown with vulture's wings
To the edge of the sky?
Have you sung with the sparrows
In the beginning of daylight
Or hooted with the owls
In the midst of the night?
Have you sprinted like an ostrich
At 40 miles an hour
At 7 feet tall, and 12 inch eggs
You would have a lot of power
Has your heart raced like a hummingbird
At hundreds of beats a minute
Such a small creature, so delicate
But a strong heart to fit it
Have you waddled like a penguin
In a world full of ice
To us it sounds so unpleasant
But to them a joy to life
Have you ever had the graciousness
And beauty of a swan
So protective from anyone
Who tries to hurt their young
Have you ever cooed
Like a pigeon or a dove
Their sounds are so beautiful
What's not to love
Have you ever talked like a parrot
And been the first parrot to talk
As for the peoples first reaction
They were probably the ones to squawk
Have you flown with the geese
In groups down south
They know winter is coming by instinct
Not by word of mouth

> >

90

Many kinds of birds
On land or in the sky
Please hoot or chirp
And let me know you're nearby

~ ~ ~

7TH GRADE SILVER MEDAL AWARD
Juliet Freudman
Great Neck North Middle School, Great Neck, NY

Pedro

When I wake up
He is mushy
When I go to school
He waits for me
And wags his tail when I come home
When I'm with him
I feel so unafraid
When I see him
I feel so happy
His wet nose
His soft, black fur
He's Pedro
He loves to play in the snow and in the lake
I see a speck of white on his chest
And some brown in his beard
Besides that, this dog is fully black
This mass of black fur is extra mushy in the mornings

He has his high bark
That's for attention
He has his low, growly bark
That's for strangers walking by our house
He has his small bark
That's to use the bathroom
He loves to use that in the middle of the night
He has another growl
But that's when he's playing

> >

My favorite noise that he makes
Is his beautifully, arched tail slapping against the wall with happiness

When he doesn't get groomed
His bangs cover his dark eyes
The long fur is soft, warm, and extra mushy

As a wise man once quoted,
"His nose is the most fascinating part of his body,
The most powerful sense.
The nasal passage is longer than ours,
And at the end is a truffle of a nose."
It can be compared to a vacuum cleaner
Sweeping things up as it sniffs over the ground
In the morning,
It's dry and warm
Later in the day,
It gets wet and cold

"Poodies!" someone cries out
He runs!
He wants to play
He sniffs
And marks his territory

Although not a kisser
He couldn't love us more
No other dog can compare
They all stare with insane jealousy
Because they all wish they had a dog like mine
He's my best friend
And no matter how old he gets
He will always be my puppy

7TH GRADE BRONZE MEDAL AWARD

Alex Feinstein
Oceanside Middle School, Oceanside, NY

The Penalty Shot

The referee drops the black biscuit onto the dot.
He signals the goalie to get ready for the shot.

The goalie waves his big glove in the air.
Bangs his stick against the net, checking it's there.

Then he glides quickly to a stop.
He crouches in his stance in the crease at the top.

He guides his wooden stick into place,
With a focused look upon his face.

The player begins his penalty shot by starting to skate,
Pushing off his right foot, then left, so fast he can't wait.

The goalie fakes him to commit to a shot as part of the fight.
Handling the puck with his stick, the player moves right.

He leaves himself open on his right glove side,
The player pushes the puck to that spot making it glide.

He fakes the shot to the blocker then shoots glove side right.
Where two posts meet, with all of his might.

The goalie pretends he won't make it in time,
Then pushes off extending his glove as the puck starts to climb.

The puck finds its way into the glove; his team thinks it's nice,
As the angry player slams his stick on the ice.

The goalie smiles as he looks up at the scores,
When he says, "Nice try, but my goal's to deny yours!"

TJ Buttgereit
W. Tresper Clarke Middle School, Westbury, NY

The World to Day

The world today is hectic
Our minds are so infected
Peace is out of reach
But when darkness has breached
Hope does not retreat
Goodness shines
A newborn baby is a sign
That love is alive

~ ~ ~

Yinny Chan
Great Neck North Middle School, Great Neck, NY

The Truth

Something you can run from,
But not hide from

Something you can try to forget,
But not ignore

The truth,
Will always be around the corner

It's time to face it,
It's time to know it

Keep running,
But it'll always be right behind you

Ryan Connors
Woodland Middle School, East Meadow, NY

I Am

I am Ryan Connors
I wonder what the war in Iraq looks like.
I hear the call of the soldiers coming home.
I see them marching home.
I want them to live.
I am Ryan Connors

I pretend that it's fake.
I feel them not enjoying the war.
I touch the desert-like sands.
I worry if they will make it home.
I cry if they don't come back.
I am Ryan Connors

I understand Obama's wish for them to come back.
I say "I agree" a lot.
I dream them coming home.
I try to help them.
I hope they live.
I am Ryan Connors

Jasmine Hakimian
Great Neck North Middle School, Great Neck, NY

You are a Butterfly

Take a look at a butterfly,
And what is it that you see,
A creature with wings, just passing by,
Or a symbol of peace, hope, a showing of beauty.

To me this living delicacy is both,
Not only these characteristics a butterfly holds,
For a butterfly is also a sign of growth,
Similar to a human and precious like gold.

For when a butterfly is born,
At its first peek at the world,
When its shell is no longer worn,
You feel like you've found a pearl.

A butterfly is unique, also representing diversity,
Each one is differently beautiful, none are the same,
Different stripes, colors, patterns, but each is meant to be,
For each has a purpose, a goal, an aim.

Realize the resemblance between a butterfly and yourself,
How everyone and everything is unique and special,
How no one should feel bad about themselves,
How both humans and butterflies are so delicate like crystals,
How precious we are,
How we should make the best of life,
How we're each our own star,
And should appreciate our lives,
How we should always keep a smile on our faces,
And always be proud,
Through ages and ages,
So say it aloud.

Take a look at a butterfly,
And what is it that you see,
A creature with wings, just passing by,
Or a symbol of peace, hope, a showing of beauty.

Jo Klein
W. Tresper Clarke Middle School, Westbury, NY

Behind These Walls

Behind these walls everything changes
Nothing is the same
People may make fun of me thinking it's a game
But I think differently behind these walls

Behind these walls everything turns to black
You can't see my true colors
You can't go forward you can't go back
You may think you know me
But you don't behind these walls

Behind these walls I can't think straight
It's like I'm trapped in my own fate
I can't find out what's real or fake
I'm feeling so different like there's an earthquake
Nothing will feel the same way it did behind these walls

I'm not sure how I felt before
I'm not sure how I feel anymore
I can move I can walk I can run but the worst part is that I can't hide
I want to know what it's like outside
But I can't get out from behind these walls

Behind these walls I can't see anyone's faces
I can't go anywhere like any new places
I'm stuck in this place not knowing where I am
All these ideas are trapped in my head
But I can't show them behind these walls

Behind these walls is where I'll always be
I'll never get out I'll never be free
So I'll spend my time as well as I can
Behind These Walls

Kamla Kumar
Great Neck North Middle School, Great Neck, NY

Only Human

We stare out the window
The world stares back
We are not alone
We are not alone

We love to be happy
We love to be powerful
We love to be loved

We fear standing out
We fear standing up
We fear taking a stand at all

We stare out the window
The world stares back
We are not alone
We are not alone

We feel anger when not included
We feel anger when we are at fault
We feel anger just to feel anger

We hate the possibility of ourselves failing
We hate the possibility of others succeeding
We hate the possibility of being only human

We stare out the window
The world stares back
We are not alone
We are not alone

We want to be right
We want to be the best
We want to be number one

We need attention
We need support
We need help

> >

We stare out the window
The world stares back
We are not alone
We are not alone

We love
We fear
We feel anger
We hate
We want
We need
We are only human

We stare out the window
The world stares back
We are not alone
We were never alone

Briana Lunn
Great Neck North Middle School, Great Neck, NY

Homeless in the Winter

It's not easy being homeless in the winter.
The sky gets dark early,
Although the city lights light up the night.
She never knows what's coming.

The trees are bare and frozen
Just like that little girl.
Except for the fact,
Trees don't shiver.

The falling rain is like the tears streaming down her face.
She's crying from fear and sadness.
There's no roof over her head to keep her dry,
Besides the stores' awnings.

If there were a place to go, she'd go.
For now, she sits, cries, and shivers.
Just like the trees and the rain.
It's not easy being homeless in the winter.

~ ~ ~

Tristyn Arcadia Mandel
Great Neck South Middle School, Great Neck, NY

White

I am a timid voice that whispers, barely heard in the distance
Symbolic of surrender a flag dancing in the breeze
A fluffy feather of a dove peacefully gliding through the air
Blending in with the wall, my wisdom forms a blank stare
I am the porcelain skin of a newborn baby
A bright hopeful light at the end of a dark tunnel
Decorative foam on thrashing ocean waves
I say nothing yet I imply everything
I am white, powerfully silent

Lauren Shaoul
Great Neck North Middle School, Great Neck, NY

I Appreciate You Now

I am sorry for never acknowledging you
Sorry you never got a thank you
You went out in the cold
You worked hard everyday
You did whatever it took
You cared about my well being

You were selfless and loving
Always concerned about me
I'm sorry it took me so long
But I appreciate you now
I appreciate you now

Solomon C. Shapiro
Great Neck North Middle School, Great Neck, NY

I Love Video Games

Video games are a part of me
And I love to play the Wii.
While I am on level four
I beg my parents to let me play more.
But whenever I die in the game
I fall out of my perfect domain.

My favorite game is World Tour
But some people think it is a real bore.
I also play James Bond
A game of which I'm really fond.
I have a game called Trigger Man
In which to win you need to have a plan.

I also own an X-box
Which I think kind of rocks.
Even though the controllers are not wireless
When I play I am always tireless.
And when I play it with my friends
The fun never ends.

And when I play games of war
They always have lots of blood and gore.
Some days I always like to play
No matter what anyone ever tries to say.
So on a day that it is raining
I will always be inside gaming.

Briana Susino
St. Thomas the Apostle School, West Hempstead, NY

This is Goodbye

I don't know how to say this,
I don't know what to do,
But you have no clue what I am going through.

You are like one in a million, but the most special one
Your beautiful smile was as bright as the sun,
Whenever I tried to read a book,
I just kept dreaming of how you look.

You were my everything, you were my all
Being without you is like taking a fall.
All I ever wanted was to be in your heart,
And for us to be together and never apart.

Now time has gone by with smiles and tears
The times I will remember for years and years.
Now I am here with a confession to make
Breaking our hearts, like cutting a cake.

So I am not going to pretend
I am heartbroken once again.
I think it's time to take a break,
I just hope what I'm doing is not a mistake.

So if you are wondering why
I don't really have a reply.
I hope you don't cry,
But this is my goodbye.

Kara Zielinski
Oceanside Middle School, Oceanside, NY

My Music

The zipper unzips and the Velcro pulls away
I open the case
Out comes my musical instrument
The violin

I check the tuning and tighten my bow
I go into position
The conductor cues us and it starts

My fingers fly
My bow joins the fun
Off we are playing
Faster and
Faster and
Faster

We get louder
Then softer
Then loud again

Suddenly the song is done
No more fingers and bows flying
No more music
The fun stops and there is silence
Then we get cued again and…

The fun begins again!!!

8TH GRADE

Amanda Chambers
Woodland Middle School, East Meadow, NY

Their Last Day

They spent the day together
And wished it would last forever

Reality was something they had to face
But their last day did not go to waste

For he will be gone tomorrow
So tonight they'll share their sorrows

"And even though we'll be miles apart,
You'll always be in my heart."

He whispers in her ear
The night before he will disappear

Morning comes and she begs him to stay
"Please don't go away."

He wipes the tears from her eyes
As they say their good-byes

"I'm leaving for Iraq,
But don't worry; I'll be back."

He's going to fight in a war
And she cries as he walks out the door

She walks upstairs and hugs his old T-shirt
She feels so hurt

She is fragile, but she will not break
She tries to smile but knows that it's fake

She believes she'll see him soon
And prays he'll get to see his baby turn one in June

And that last day they spent together,
She knew it couldn't last forever.

8TH GRADE SILVER MEDAL AWARD

Ariel Gourdet
Sewanhaka High School, Floral Park, NY

The Day

Everyone's waiting,
for her to come down.
Squirming impatiently in their seats.
They wait.
The music has started,
and down she comes
in her long white dress.
She's walking down the aisle,
with her head up high,
carrying her flowers,
with such pride.
On the other end
they wait for her arrival.
This is her first wedding,
and she can feel their eyes on her.
At first she was nervous,
but the nerves have escaped her.
She's trying her hardest
not to hurry,
since there's no need to rush.
As she approaches the end,
a weight has been lifted.
Almost instantly,
everyone stands and turns around
to watch the bride
walk down the trail of flowers
the flower girl left behind.

Brenna Riordan
Oceanside Middle School, Oceanside, NY

A Friend

A friend is always there to help before you fall through the cracks.
Just like a shadow they follow when you need it most.
When they stay after you reject them and misunderstand their
actions of love, they prove themselves a true friend.

A friend is the first glimpse of sunlight after a hurricane rips
through your life and destroys everything, the first drop of rain
after an overwhelming drought, and the last soldier to return home
from war unharmed.

A friend is someone who walks away from it all, the pretender friends,
popularity, fame or fortune to tell you everything will be okay.
Without considering every odd against you a friend believes in you
when the world is against you. This friend chases away the rain
when you're waiting on a rainbow.

But most of all, a friend will be ringing your doorbell in their pajamas
with a carton of ice cream to help you remember how to smile.

Melinda Calderon
Woodland Middle School, East Meadow, NY

Life

Should I know the wisdom I do?
I'm so young
Yet feel so old

My heart,
Like the oldest tortoise
Sees things
That others
Do not, or will not see

Like the way the air
Plays tag with the tousles
Of green and brown
That are the old,
Ancient,
Trees

Or the beautiful,
Hypnotic dance
That the wind and rain
Perform with the loud voice of the thunder
And the pretty face of lightning
To make the show
Even more beautiful

I wonder why
Not even the smartest, or witty of us
Don't take time
To look around this wonderful,
Wonderful present of a world
That has been given to us

We won't live forever
I've already found this out
I strive to remind myself

> >

That life is the sweetest of fruits
That will go rotten,
If not eaten soon.

~ ~ ~

Kiaya Rose Dilsner-Lopez
Oceanside Middle School, Oceanside, NY

The Tree Stump

In front of my house was a dead tree
In spring, the leaves did not sprout
In summer, the leaves did not radiate
And in autumn, the leaves did not change color and fall
There were no leaves, so we declared the tree to be dead.

One morning, I awoke to a noise
It was the noise of the tree being killed even though it was already dead.
My sister also awoke
And she became upset

The people that were killing the dead tree
Left a stump for her
Which I later found out meant:
        Less work for them
        And the world to my sister

She played with the stump
Sat on it, stood on it
Jumped on it, lay on it
Pretended on it, imagined on it

Now in front of my house is an awkward stump
It does not suit the appearance of the house
Some people would remove it
But we won't until it rots
But once it does, then the stump will be gone
And nothing will mark the grave of the once alive tree.

Jennifer Ferrante
Portledge School, Locust Valley, NY

Mother Earth

The scent of pine engulfs the quaint log cabin
Neatly standing nestled among the sea of green

I inhale the calm and tranquil air
Taking it in while there is still time

Maple trees producing sap thick and sweet as sugar
Syrup that tastes good drenched atop anything

Blue jays singing their infinite lullabies
Hypnotizing creatures all around

All stop their busy days-
Bees shush their buzzing and observe

Flowers that normally stretch with the sun aren't quite so rigid,
They stop obeying their commander star and float a minute on the gentle
breeze

Songs so serene and graceful
Gents calling to the lady birds, flying away together towards the heavens

I inhale the calm and tranquil air
Taking it in while there is still time

For far away trees are cut, chopped, slashed
No regard for nature in the least

Remember the lazy mornings
Waking up to rocking on the porch sipping fresh tea on ice

Preserve the crisp fresh springs that run through like veins of the woods
Keeping alive shrubs and animals all around

Carelessness of man is forcing the forests to thin air
Springs polluted and irreversibly poisoned

> >

We must do something to ensure that posterity gets a chance to view the
natural world
Youth grows up on video games and radio news

Inhale the calm and tranquil air
Take it in while there is still time

Our carelessness and disregard for mother
Crippling and paralyzing her

Whatever seems more convenient at the second is what we revert to
If it means dumping wastes into the early ancient oceans, we will

Sands in an hourglass eventually grovel to the bottom
No being can stop it; Time is not forever

We are killing our creator
Only to further convenience ourselves

There is no denying and little time for trying
Heal the mother, she is dying

~ ~ ~

Cody Goldsmith
Oceanside Middle School, Oceanside, NY

You look in her eyes.
As sharp as a tack,
she turns around and gives you her back.
No time to talk.
Never around.
Looking at her, not even a sound.
She likes to play,
real hard to get.
She looks in your eyes, with no regret.
You turn away,
not even a sound.
She looks away,
she turns around.
She catches a glimpse,
in the corner of her eye.

>>

She never talks, when you're nearby.
She looks away, you take the walk.
No more games, how about we talk?

~ ~ ~

Anna Harsham
Sewanhaka High School, Floral Park, NY

Always here

Why are you crying?
I haven't left you yet
I am here for the time being
Just be thankful for now
Don't think of what is coming
Still remember I love you
Still remember we can always talk
Even if I am on the other side

Why are you crying?
Your tears should be of joy
I won't have to endure this much longer
Be happy for me!
I will be with God
We will see each other again
When you come to stay with me...

I see that you are still crying
I've been gone for awhile
You should forget me
Just stay away for awhile
Maybe you will feel better
I know that I do
I am here with God
You will be here later
But for now your tears will not resurrect me
So don't cry anymore
I've left life for good
You can visit me when you are done mourning
My loss that just isn't worth it

Just stop crying over my grave
You're bringing back the pain
Of what was happening before
Please be happy for me
I will be here when you come
Don't be sad for me
I am ok now
Just remember
I will always be here with God

~ ~ ~

Caroline Juang
Manhasset Middle School, Manhasset, NY

Aboard a Dream

Down in the woods, all dark at night,
Somehow I found myself at the door of a shack
A shack so gloomy, I quivered with fright
So I turned and ran, never looking back.

Out into the bright sunshine, there I flew
Like a bird with bright plume, I sailed in the sky
Even though it was night, the day seemed anew
Flying to sea, but never knowing why.

I landed on a bright turquoise ship
In the middle of the shining Pacific sea
The water looked as if I could take a sip
While gulls overhead chattered at me.

Soon I was swimming in the middle of a pond
Rainbow scales lined my sides
Fish darted past me, then swam into the beyond
I flicked my tail and went along for the ride.

> >

114

Now I was riding in the street
Past pedestrians walking slower than me
My eyes were headlights, and tires were my feet
Then I waited for a light to turn green.

In a haunted mansion I floated and then
My surroundings turned black and I heard a scream
In broad daylight I jolted out of bed
Realizing that my mind before was just aboard a dream.

~ ~ ~

Tristynn Mercedes
W. Tresper Clarke Middle School, Westbury, NY

Garbage Monster

There is a chore
That I hate even more
It is the stinkiest one of them all
Doing this chore
Makes my nose and eyes sore
With the stench that makes me cry
It is so bad I want to die
But it is an obligation
To my nation
To keep my house clean
Otherwise we might as well lie
On a stinky pile of rotten turkey and bread rye
It churns my gut
To hear the door shut
While my mother yelling "Take out the trash!"
It makes me want to crash into the floor
For the stench is truly sickening
As my heart starts quickening
I get prepared to face the monster
OF THE TRASH!!!!

Sara Pepkin
Plainedge Middle School, Bethpage, NY

She Walks

She looks around
and makes no sound, but
She walks.

Even though she knows
she's got nowhere to go,
She walks.

Cars whiz by,
she hasn't got a try, but
She walks.

People stare
but she doesn't care and
She walks.

She knows God's on her side,
so she keeps her head up with pride and
She walks.

Stephanie Pierre
St. Thomas the Apostle School, West Hempstead, NY

Realize

Black is Black
White is White
Life is always
A racial fight.

Don't date her
Don't marry him.
He doesn't match
The color of your skin.
Why does it matter?
Why do we care?
Would you see a difference
If skin wasn't there?

They may use a language
We do not speak
They may have beliefs
We find unique.
But deep down inside
Beneath that thin shell,
You may just find someone
You know very well.

Friends come in all sizes, colors, and shapes,
And you might miss a lot
If you only see a face.
Each culture has something
Unique we can learn
To make our lives better,
Our souls much more pure.
So cast off your prejudice
Replace hate with love
And look after each other
Like the Father above.

Adanilsy Polanco
Weldon E. Howitt Middle School, Farmingdale, NY

Any Day Holiday

I didn't have a big red bow.
I didn't have a Christmas tree.
I didn't have a birthday cake.
But you came in anyway.

Your smile was the biggest.
Your laugh was the loudest.
Your hugs were the warmest.
You painted my life with swirls of color.

There was no shiny wrapping paper,
Gleaming beneath the holiday lights.
You came wrapped in smiles and questions,
With hugs and laughs on top.

You were one of a kind
Made especially for me
You beat the competition.

Being my best life term investment.
Like the shiny new bike for every eight-year old boy
And that beautiful doll for the girl next door
You were the gift that needed no holiday

The one you can't grow out of with time
On my any day holiday
You were the gift that surpassed the years
And brought yourself to the top of my tree
And into my heart.

Nicolette Robinson
Alverta B. Gray Schultz Middle School, Hempstead, NY

your eyes!

when I gaze into your eyes
I see the sun rise I feel the sun shine
your eyes take me away
to a place where there's no trouble
where there's no fighting
to a place where I have no fears
to a place where there's blue skies
and beautiful beaches

your eyes bring me joy
they melt my heart like no other
especially when
we stare at each other

your eyes give me butterflies
you make me nervous
whenever I look at you
it makes me want to blurt out
"I love you!"
I understand that you might love another
the truth
I just want you to be happy

your eyes bring me joy
they melt my heart like no other
especially when
we stare at each other

you're the one that makes me
want to see the sun rise
each and every time I gaze into your ...

I bet even Columbus with a compass
        could get lost in your
                Eyes!

Ariel Sobel
South Woods Middle School, Syosset, NY

My First Slow Dance

The music was so light it was barely even there
I was in a daydream – unprepared
Yet I came across a new, different kind of stare
As your eyes met mine I saw colors gleam
Your words galloped towards my heart as if in a dream
Best friends forever is not the kind of friends it seems
You sweetly asked, "Will you dance with me?"
I wasn't used to the music, but I nodded with great glee
This was the boy I've always loved, but did he feel the same for me?
My stomach twirled just like I as we glided to the floor
The soft charming music came alive although it was once a bore
Maybe it was time for something fresh, something more
He put his hand in mine, mine in his
And as we wobbled I craved his gentle kiss
But I knew it was for another day, so kept it as a wish
You beckoned me to turn, so I swirled round and round
Who knew till I was dizzy and lost, I would be found?
You held me close, as if I'd run away
But I'll save that catastrophe for another day
The music stopped, but not us looking in each other's eyes
So, on my first dance I did not dance but instead fly.

9TH GRADE

Evelyn Weinstein
Roslyn High School, Roslyn Heights, NY

The Scholar at Sea

The scholar searches for an ancient gleam
Glimpsed only now and then through pages
The glow of fascination, beauty
Only in words, in ink
For him.

The sky, the heaving sea
Slow bitter burning of the stars
He can no longer see
Except in language.

He does not move from his place by the candle
Though the terrible roar of the sea
And the groan of the thrashing ship
Are loud and vivid, he cannot grasp them.

He hears the words.
The words are his.

No natural beauty is true for him
Except through the lens of another's mind
Even when the wind roars
And the dark water rages in mountains
And his ship cowers before the storm
He is not stirred;

No, not even the sea anymore
Holds life for him.
He remains below deck,
Lost to everything–

Except the words.

Amanda Carr
Herricks High School, New Hyde Park, NY

Searching

A small boy stands
in the middle of town.
His hands held tall
and motionless above his head.
He looks around, searching
for the rounded tan face of his mother.
He looks to the right,
and instantly his minute body
is filled with terror.
The dark horrid eyes
of a soldier connect with his.
The soldier looks like
a hawk staring him down.

Then the boy searches to the left.
Tears begin to gradually crawl
down the side of his face.
Where has his mother gone?

The soldiers start to walk around.
Circling the townspeople,
like they were lions
hunting down their prey.
As one of them approaches,
the small boy gasps deeply out of anxiety.
The soldier then passes,
and the bewildered, frightened
little boy exhales.
Maybe they will not take him away today.
But where is his mother?

At last the soldiers demand
them to lower their arms.
As the boy turns back to the right,
he spots his mother.
Her tanned skin shiny, and tear stained.
Today they are safe,
and still together.

Sohum Patwa
Herricks High School, New Hyde Park, NY

Deuce

My eyes are the dry lines of a tennis court
Which show no mercy
When choosing the winner.

My ears are nothing more
Than the sound of a tennis ball;
Crisply bouncing off the clay.

My deft hands are the strings;
Effortlessly whisking away
Every ball I meet.

My body is the net
Permitting nothing
Through my barriers.

My heart is the witness
Of the years
Of broken racquets,
Of broken spirits.

But perhaps I was once the player,

Who had seen the lines,
Heard the ball,
Overcome the net,
And become the racquet?

Arianna Bombardiere
Herricks High School, New Hyde Park, NY

I Wear My Brain On My Back

I don't recall wearing a heart on my sleeve, but a brain on my back
where all of it goes, but no one ever knows

wouldn't it be insensible, to keep my brain in my head?

where every conflict would have to be solved
every past disappointment would be brought up

again, and
again, and
again

if my brain's on my back, I can simply avoid it all
it keeps at a steady flow, at a pattern that goes

problem, back, gone
problem, back, gone

silly as it seems, it seems to work for me

I keep my brain on my back
so there's not much thinking

about what someone did to me
or what they might do to me

pain in that case would be the enemy
but with my brain on my back

thinking about it,
constantly.
easily.
regrettably?

passes right over me

se Carter-Foster

_evelt High School, Roosevelt, NY

Just A Dream

Dreams can get the best of you.
Like when I dreamt you told me you fell for another person.
Good thing it's just a dream.
I dreamt feeling the pain pierce my heart like a tattoo needle.
I felt betrayal sink down into the depths of my soul.
I felt my heart drop in the pit of my stomach.
Good thing it's just a dream.
I dreamt my world flipped upside down.
Everything that was organized, flown out of place.
A hurricane of questions took over my mind.
Why couldn't I wake up from the dream?
It was a dream…right?
Everybody has dreams, but this one just won't seem to stop.
People say a dream is a wish your heart makes.
But this one couldn't come true…could it?
Good thing it's just a dream…or reality.

Sarah D'Arienzo
East Meadow High School, East Meadow, NY

Alone Shall Never Stand

In a land filled with blue wonder
Is a place I have never known
It is filled with lightning and rolling thunder
With stars that have never shone

As I walk along the ground of sand
I see prisoners that have been set free
And I long for the feel of my own land
Not these dark depths of the sea

I cannot understand their ways
For these are ones of mystery
Yet I long to stay here all of my days
For my own land has no such history

I knew my land would soon be lost
Somehow I knew there was still hope
I felt the pain and knew the cost
And with lasting faith I cope

Ever and ever will the sea stay blue
I realize that a journey is coming near
And to leave this place I never knew
Now my path becomes unclear

I stare out into the dark of night
And remember my lost land
I see a lone star shining bright
And realize forever alone shall never stand

e Gottlieb
W. Hewlett High School, Hewlett, NY

She falls from the sky
As if she descended from G-ds.
Her bright color burns my eye,
But I wish for her to come, to beat the odds
On a hot, July day.
I hope to taste her on my tongue
And watch her melt into the bay,
Disappearing with the young,
Always leaving slices of ice,
Little remnants of beauty's past;
Glistening white powder, mud-speckled like dice,
Vanishing fast
"And yet, by heaven, I think my love as rare," *
She, the snow, cannot be compared.

*William Shakespeare, Sonnet 130

~ ~ ~

Tiffany Ha
Oyster Bay High School, Oyster Bay, NY

Some days the world is a bookstore.
I am a wistful novel,
Hoping customers will read my pages,
And spend time to understand my story.
Wishing people would stop judging me by others' opinions,
And for once pick me up for who I am.

Chelsey Kim
Hicksville High School, Hicksville, NY

The Tragic Tale

Within my dream a memory laid
Beneath my eyes, an image scattered array
Shredded and torn the pieces arose
Tragic... The fairytale unfolds

Once was a princess ever so sad
The once streaming teardrops now crystallized glass
With a dead cold stoned heart
Alone she froze, face down in the dark

Delicate as the frail white rose so pure and innocent
She glared back her fears
In hopes to keep the darkness away
From those she held dear

"Mirror Mirror on the wall
Who shall be the last to fall
Broken and shattered is all I see
The imperfections found in me"

Oh, how miserable she looked
with her tear-stained face
If only she could find a
Happier place...

With a mask of fake smiles she held this disguise
Even when drowning in every tear she cried
Crawling on the floor, pulling in strain
Never did she think to show the world her pain

With time did she realize this is all she would be.
The demon within would kill her slow and sweetly
The dark corners in her heart overtook her dreams
As shadows would breathe they took the struggle
Piece by piece

> >

Buried alive she would suffocate to death
The struggle for air with every shaky gasp
How much could one soul take
Before it should break??

Held between her whispered sighs
She muttered…
A minute too late

~ ~ ~

Donna Kim
Herricks High School, New Hyde Park, NY

Bliss

My heart is fluttering,
Mesmerized by the breathtaking view.
Falling from the heavens,
Pure bliss and innocence.

Dancing in the crystal skies,
Shimmering ballerinas bow down to earth.
The alluring sight of felicity,
Cherished in every soul.

The pure, icy kisses
Send unconditional love,
Sculpting an exquisite and precise
Pure, white paradise.

Perfectly crafted, lustrous wonders
Descend with delicacy and elegance.
Heavenly snowflakes frolic,
Whispering the arrival of winter.

Michelle Leibowitz
Herricks High School, New Hyde Park, NY

If Life's a Stage, Then I'm a Good Actress

Find me a book
About a 13-year-old girl
Who can never live up
To expectations
Who lost her passion for the future
Years after proving hers
Whose layers of bliss are thin but plentiful
Transparent in her eyes
Who's frustrated at home
And needs to, yet can't get away
Who few people listen to
"She's so cute, she's always happy"
Who never gets mad
Because she's too numb to care
Who cares
More than she should?
Whose innocent ways
Is a role to cover what she knows
Who can't accept
Knows, but refuses
Who's talked about
Though her intentions are good
Who's tried everything "bad" she possibly could
Just to feel
Who wants nothing more
But to go back and change who she became
Who looks vulnerable
Plays strong
Who's been used
And still trusts
Who's been through enough to know what's wrong
But is too inexperienced to care
I doubt you could find a book
Exactly like
The story I live

1 School, Oyster Bay, NY

Some days, the world is a forest-
I am an enduring oak.
My branches held high in the face of doubts;
My roots deep underground, set to never let go
The bark on my body will not shed-
The leaves on my limbs will not fall.
I am the tree that will not bow.
I am the tree that will not fade.

Christina Pil
Great Neck North High School, Great Neck, NY

Nature's Sorrows

The little child
Faced with the burden of the sea
Controlling to his slightest whim
Showing his anger and happiness
With the crashing waves or calming ripples.

His leisure only with the wonders of the sea
Which he had grew too accustomed
And in his fury at his boredom,
Bring his waves as high as he can
Hoping again and again
But never seems to touch the sky.

A young maiden
Twirling in the ivory rugs set on the ground.
With her smile, the sun glows
Yet her cries soaked up by the rugs
Drowning the world beneath
As she finds out joy will only last for a moment.
She dances in anguish, her arms swirling around her
Letting a single tree blow slightly

The old spirit in the tall knotted oak tree
Watching the world pass around him.
As life begins and ends,
A rhythm he watched in his immortality.

Flowers, underneath his caring arms
Making him smile for once,
Withering away with the cold breeze
Again his tears, his leaves, slowly trickle down.

Sunrise and sunset
Spring, Summer, Fall, Winter.
He ponders when it will finally end
As he watches life's never ending cycle.

How I See The World

The sun dances,
the bird sings,
the eagle soars and spreads its wings.
The stars glisten,
the moon glows,
This is how I see the world.

The wind whispers,
a secret it knows,
it gets around,
it goes and goes.
The true meaning,
nobody knows,
This is how I see the world.

The trees swaying,
side to side,
the leaves take off,
set out in stride.
On a journey,
they don't know why,
This is how I see the world.

The clouds hovering
overhead,
look no further, look ahead.
Far and wide, thick and spread,
This is how I see the world.

The water falls,
the mountains gaze,
the distant calls,
the forest, a maze.
Yearning for the coming days,
This is how I see the world.

Over everything,
the water flows,

> >

the trees shake,
the rooster crows,
our time is up, the final blows.
This is how I see the world.

Newborn baby as I leave,
I'm still alive, I still believe.
My soul lives on within this girl,
This is how I see the world.
This is how I see the world.

~ ~ ~

Julie Titus
Herricks High School, New Hyde Park, NY

A Friend

Over the hundreds of pinky promises
The thousands of shake hands.
Millions of smiles shared,
And laughs, existing forever.

The tears never forgotten, and
Times spent together.
All stored, not in any USB
But in the heart.

A shoulder to lean on
Or even 24/7 of open arms.
Entitled to us.
Priceless.

Do they all come in small packages
wrapped on top with a red ribbon?
Unfortunately not.
Picked amongst the countless
specks of sand.

Much more precious than
Silver or gold.
Bringing a smile to everyone.

10TH GRADE

10TH GRADE GOLD MEDAL AWARD

Hara Prager
Portledge School, Locust Valley, NY

```
                    The sky
                was gray, the air
             stingy and cold. Soon my
             mind inwardly began to
             fold. I glanced quickly
                   from left to right,
                   and then I
                   looked be-
         hind. Nobody... I was alone...Just me
        and my mind, playing tricks on me again,
        I thought, as I drew my coat near. There's no-
   body but      the wind, nobody to fear.  I glanced
   quickly fr    om left to right, and then I    looked
   behind.         Nobody...I was alone...Just   me and
   my mind.      I continued down the deso-       late
   street,       the rhythmic crunch of leav-    es ben-
   eath my       feet. And there it was again,   that vo-
   ice had         returned, sending a wave of     panic
   through         me that burned. I glanced     quickly
   from         left to right, and then I looked  behind.
   No-          body...I was alone...Just me        and
                my mind. As    if formed from
                the mist that  hung low arou-
                nd the trees,  he appeared.
                This shadowy,    transparent
                figure who     portrayed every-
                thing I feared. I glanced quick-
              ly from left     to right and
              then I looked       behind...
              I was never         alone ...
            He was always        with me.
            The daemon          of my mind
```

137

Sophie Azran
Manhasset High School, Manhasset, NY

Marie

Her flat topaz eyes stare at me across the room.
They don't see me; they're only glancing.
She doesn't know much of anything;
not the date, not her story,
not the reason why she's like this.

People say she's a blank piece of paper
because of her medical condition.
She's a full diary glossed over with an eraser.
They don't know how she got it;
the dementia, the depression,
the sole cause of why she doesn't recognize my face.

She loved him so much, my grandpa.
She must have, or she wouldn't be this vacant.
The end of him was the beginning of her impairment.
She saw no purpose in living;
no clothing was comfortable, no food left her satisfied.
She was the victim of her own mourning.

For so many years I have been too young
to see what was happening to the warm face,
the caring eyes, and the loving smile I once knew.
Now I have grown, and she has aged;
her cold hands, her faded golden hair,
and an expression of woe all replace who she was.

These two visages are so clear in my mind;
polar opposites, yet facets of the same personality.
Day by day her once glowing personality fades like an antique picture.
She's like the city of Pompeii,
destroyed, simply ruins,
and wearing away by the second.

Jessica Lemons
Herricks High School, New Hyde Park, NY

My Water

I can't say that I regret
The water
That I poured
Beneath the cold, stone bridge.

It ran down the river
Across a meadow of poppy flowers,
Snaked around spouts of lava
Alongside the mountains of the West,
Beneath the bridges of others
Into the horizon
And into the ocean.

And one day the water
Will return to me,
Purified and renewed.

But until it slips
Between my fingers
And drips from my hair
And slides down my face,
I can only attempt to recall
The love I felt-
Of cleanliness
Of purity
Of life-
That the water gave to me.

So I will sit on this bridge
This cold, stone bridge
As I have sat each and every day
Waiting and breathing
In a seemingly rhythmic manner
And in the distance
I will see
My water coming back to me.

Elyssa Abuhoff
John F. Kennedy High School, Plainview, NY

The Tale of Man and Land

The wind whispered the stories of the world
in my eager ears.
It told me fading tales of Man and Land through the
eyes of the mountains.
It told of how the soil has endured the
wrath of man's heel,
pressing into the virgin lands,
effacing their innocent beauty,
and raping them of their earthly riches
while leaving their steel signature in the dust.
But with the destruction,
the mountains have also witnessed
benevolent smiles
and kind eyes leading to souls
yearning for prosperity and peaceful progress;
and the mountains have seen the binding handshakes of
rainbow hands
and the knowing nods of
rainbow faces
who live for the Earth and the restoration and preservation of its beauty.
And so the wind whispered the stories of the world
in my eager ears.
It told me fading tales of Man and Land,
and as I listened,
with my mind opened to a vast expanse of wisdom,
I understood the wind's fervent message.
And so I shouted the stories of the world
to the people who had become lost within it;
to the people who could not open their minds and
hear the whispers of the wind.
And I told them fading tales of
Man and Land.

Melissa Bergersen
Herricks High School, New Hyde Park, NY

Barriers

He picked me up from
my friend's house.
I thought I had told
Mom to come.

There, in his black, gloomy truck
he waited.
I wanted to get out the
second I stepped in.

Silence all around us;
not even the distraction of the radio.
He drove,
and I stared out the window.

My hand on the
door handle
the entire ride home.

I could see the
empty space between us
growing larger with each turn of the tires.

We had invisible barriers
that were never crossed
and never would be, I feared.

Alani Grandison
Hicksville High School, Hicksville, NY

Forever I Will

Arms of ribbons wrapped around my fragile body.
He embraces my soul with the warmth of his hugs.
The love he shares pours from his heart into mine.
Allowing me to feel what I never felt before.
Awaking my fragile bones from their dreadful dreams of pain.
No longer will my back hunch over as if I was to break down piece by piece.
My head has risen to stare into the eyes of the one who revived my lost soul.
His kisses have given me life.
No longer will my skin look as if darkness has been my eternal home.
Then his lips speak of words I've heard before.
But never felt in such a way he has allowed me to experience.
These words are left lingering in my ear...
I love you forever and forever I will...

Kuldeep Singh Hare
Sewanhaka High School, Floral Park, NY

Imagination

With this I could soar over the highest peaks and through the smallest valleys
I could play with a giant squid or ride a whale through the sky
Have adventures more dangerous than any Theseus might ever have had
and still be home in time for dinner
I could visit the Mayans and see how they created their pyramids
I could fly through space and visit Saturn planet of the sea god maybe even
ask him over for dinner
I could slay a shade like Eragon or find treasure with Jack Sparrow
I could summon Bartimeus and play cards with him or help Meggie banish
Capricorn into a book
Maybe scam fairies out of their gold like Artemis or fight alongside Arthur and
have my own accommodation at his round table
I could save the territories alongside Bobby Pendragon, swim in the ocean of
the landless planet Cloral or hunt in the jungles of Denduron, maybe even take a
visit to third earth
I could come up with an invention to make trees grow overnight with Daedelus
I could make a bridge to the moon or defeat an army of Jotuns with Thor
A boring period in I+A could fly by when your Imagination takes hold
It can create worlds beyond the average man's dreams
I could save middle earth by helping Frodo reach mount doom or prevent the
carnage at Osgiliath by warning Minas Tirith
Run with the Elves in Du Weldenvarden or mine with the Dwarfs under the
Beors
I could freeze time and stop an airplane crash
I could help Belgarion speed his way to Torak and save his world
Or travel in time and prevent the orb of Aldur from ever being stolen by Torak
If I don't like the ending to a story I can rewind and give it my own ending
I could fly across the sea and visit my cousins or fly over to area 51 and see
what's there
Or should I go to mars and see if aliens live there
Maybe go to another galaxy to see if life exists somewhere else
Lift a mountain with a finger and see if it really has roots
I could go to the future and find a cure for cancer or make an android to do my
homework for me
My imagination is limitless like time and universe; with my Imagination I could
do anything!

Martina Khalek
Farmingdale High School, Farmingdale, NY

pressure,

religion,

pressure,

glory?

pressure,

family,

pressure,

BOMB

religion-

persecuted,

glory?

yeah, right…

family-

devastated, destroyed, doomed,

the ~~life~~ a suicide bomber.

Megan Malafronte
Manhasset High School, Manhasset, NY

Global History

Skinned cowhide and Dembu log carve the detail of an African Conga drum,
Feet covered in debris left from rituals when gathered by the fire.
Crystal meth led the decrepit woman's cheekbones gaunt and numb,
Blue-coated cops arrived at her door to find she was no pathological liar.

Bob Marley's interlocked coils of dreadlocks supported his Jamaican pride,
Three little birds flew south following the Buffalo soldier to survive.
Leonardo da Vinci created textiles using charcoal along each side,
Voltaire's French Enlightened philosophy continues to stay alive.

Guitarras de España played by a mariachi band thru a Mediterranean night,
Save Darfur, prevent the genocide and global warming before it kills.
Child labor continues to affect the innocent, breaking backs without a fight,
Agonized men roll dice, deal cards and play the slots building up the bills.

Peppery colored pigeons scavenge the lonesome benches of Central Park,
Lawyers dressed in exclusive Armani suits arrive to court to get paid by the hour.
Scotland cathedrals designed in Gothic style let their high ceilings dim dark,
Adolf Hitler caused the Holocaust with his dictating, gruesome power.

Superman climbed out of the New York Times comic strip to save the world,
Rickety tickety tock, who broke grandfather's clock?
JonBenet Ramsey stepped center stage in flamboyance parading locks of
        golden curls,
Back in psychedelic '69 Woodstock left hippies youth movements in musical
        shock.

Drug Free week concluded to more teenagers becoming sexually active,
Warner Brothers Pictures presents the facets of our world now and then.
Will this historical context influence dauntless humans to let peace live?
Imagine burning the Eiffel Tower and changing back time on Big Ben.

Megan Mullaney
Sewanhaka High School, Floral Park, NY

What it's Like

it's like
being the black crayon in a box of Crayola crayons.

it's like
being a freshman on the varsity team.

it's like
being 12 at a sweet 16.

it's like
being stranded in a different country other than your own.

…now that's what it's like…
to be in high school.

Samantha Penninipede
W. Tresper Clarke High School, Westbury, NY

Sunset Masterpiece

Shades of reds, oranges, and yellows,
Swirl and combine to form a whole new masterpiece.
Their easel is the sky above,
Their viewers: people like you and me.

When the sun is beginning to feel hazy,
And it drops down to where the land meets the sky,
It stops for one last check on the world,
And its colors mix together, producing a new shade.

It is seemingly day, not quite night,
Yet neither of the two.
A whole new time of day:
Not dusk, or sunrise, nor twilight.

Something that cannot be reproduced,
By an aspiring artist and claimed as their own.
No, something that can never be redone.
Yet something that will always be true.

As I come home from the day's activities,
The sun bids me adieu.
With one last wink, it sinks into the Earth,
To sleep undisturbed until the morning light.

Alicia Robinson
Freeport High School, Freeport, NY

Silence

Abandonment surrounds my self inflicted solitude
Bearing down on my sanity, a light of exigency
Closes in on me, humiliating my barren shelter
Deviating me from the silence I drown myself in
Establishing my soul in a glass cage, translucent so
Foes can't come through, but be able to see the truth
Getting to know me in sinless silence
Hovering over the steep cliff not wanting to dive
Into the indisputable truth
Jumping into what might kill me, but save me
Kneeling under the pressure to be perfect
Lovelorn feeling creeps behind my still ears seeping through my skin into
My malcontented, malignant, maddened heart
Neutrality is what I bask in, when my sanity is at war
Overthrown by this quiet that heals my bleeding soul so silently
Pantomimist looks flow from my body as I
Quietly, I take the time to gather my conscience and
Reach for an opportunity to break this
Silence that secludes and dictates a voice of reticence
Takes over and titles my book of life
Untitled and it umbrages me leaving me to
Vacant dark corners of civilization
Walls surround me in vast open spaces
Xenophobic feelings encase me in a hollow life of
Yammering silence …
Zero existence; Zero feeling; Zero emotion
Captured
In
Silence …

Amanda Simms
Farmingdale High School, Farmingdale, NY

Darkness surrounds her as the
Tide swiftly changes once more.
The waves of realization,
Which had only lapped at her before,
Now reached up high over her unsuspecting head with threatening force,
Pulling her deep under.

Slowly suffocating and unable to breathe,
She is engulfed by the impenetrable waters.
It would kill her to surrender, so instead she struggles,
Trying desperately to resurface.

The calm sea has quickly betrayed her.
The once serene, inviting waters are now a
Rough, impersonal ocean,
Unforgiving and relentless.
Far from the coastline, she is swept away,
Leaving anything significant in her wake.

In her moment of utter weakness,
She discovers a twisted peacefulness
As she drifts farther away from reality.
But her lungs scream in protest,
And the piercing, agonized sound ignites a spark.
And just before she collapses,
Just before she fades into blackness...

She emerges.
Gasping for air, she walks onto the beach,
Ignoring the surf that crashes mercilessly against her back.
The dawn's promising sunlight glistens upon her skin,
And she stands on the shore,
Alone again

But no longer in the dark.

Alexandra Tenenbaum
Freeport High School, Freeport, NY

My Mother
Is not the woman I aim to be.

My mother
Had a family once
A loving husband
And four young kids

But she
Burned all her bridges
Turned her back on matrimony
And forgot her four beautiful labors of love
With just a touch of help from
The white powder she sought comfort in
And the men's arms she used as her
Fire.

Mommy
Was soon nowhere to be found
Her children she claimed to be her
Good done on earth
Have scars that never heal.

They say she was once known
As mommy
And not just psycho

But I was born last
I never knew a mother
Mommy
I only knew psycho
And her warpath

She will never be
The woman, mother or
Wife I aim to be.

Caitlin Viscio
Oceanside High School, Oceanside, NY

In Memoriam

The world is aglow in hues of gold and red.
Flames threatening to engulf me.
They mimic the color rising high in my cheeks,
that virus called Denial.
I find myself numb.
Numb to everything
but the fermenting sickness inside me.

Snow falls around me
filling the gutter I sleep in
with flakes that fight the flames,
but burn my skin.

The sun peaks high in the sky
fueling the fire that rages inside me,
yet offering reprieve from the icy burns.
Melted snow puddles at my feet.

I peel back layers of clothing,
embracing the blood bubbling beneath my skin.
Accepting that you're gone.
Acceptance. I whisper the word.
The flames shrink to a dull glow
like a sunset flowing through my veins.
And I realize.
Happiness doesn't mean that I don't miss you.

11TH GRADE

11TH GRADE GOLD MEDAL AWARD

Sarah Taormino
Freeport High School, Freeport, NY

Ourglass

When   we   are   together   the
Months
Weeks
Days
Hours
Minutes
Seconds
Slip
Through
Our
Fingers
Like
Sand
And
When
We
Are
Apart
The
Seconds
Minutes
Hours
Days
Weeks
Months
Are the chains that bind me
I   long   to   break   free

Emily Mervosh
W. Tresper Clarke High School, Westbury, NY

Winter Snowflakes

For one afternoon
You allow winter
To freeze time.

Let every tiny flake of snow
Bring stress levels down a degree.
Let every glossy hill
Propel you into a school-free season.
Hope that it won't leave you
With black ice.

Gathering and organizing supplies
You put all assignments on hold,
Though you fail to forget about
Schoolwork one day.

Anxious to see friends
You remember small talk
Is not your strong point
And that it would be in your best interest
To hold off on SAT words for the day.

You focus on the task on hand
Feeling nervous, tired, stressed.
Automatically add lines and angles
To pictures in the directions.

For a moment, you substitute thought for feeling.

Dreams burst into ideas
Scissors cut swirls across
Standard copy paper.
Invisible tape holds
The edges together.

Snowflakes take shape.

> >

Markers explode in color
Brighter shades overshadowing
Darker grays and browns.
Intricate designs emerge
From random dots and lines.

You open your ears, your eyes
To Advent readings
And Christmas carols
Substitute laws of Newton
For Commandments of God.

You forget
Crammed tests, sleepless nights, strenuous papers
Bury them
In snow and marshmallows and cookie dough.

You sing, you dance, you laugh, you love.
Absorb blessings as they fall from Heaven…

The perfect snowflake hangs
In a cold empty window
The time and effort it required
Hidden from its viewers.

It revives your Christmas spirit.
It becomes a simple miracle.

It becomes your own North Star.

Rachel Sferlazza
Farmingdale High School, Farmingdale, NY

the big bad wolf loves snow white

it's your scent
drives me wild(er)
your eyes
the winter rain
your hair
the black turning ravens green
your skin
so soft, so milky
do you mind fur?

for you, i've even given up pork
since you've been so kind to me
especially after i was accused of eating that poor old grandmother
though humans taste like old shoes
i'd much rather have another little pig… oops
you drive me wild(er) sometimes

if you forget that womanizer, prince charming
choose me instead
i can guarantee you the following:
      i will always keep my fur soft
      i will always bring you home dinner (hope you like rare steaks)
      i will always feel this way about you

in a sense, you've civilized me
tamed me
but really all you've done is driven me wild(er)

Catey Appel
Jericho High School, Jericho, NY

Reflection

Within the mirror on my wall
I see a face that I recall
With thoughts beneath it sadly blurred
Among the raging teenage herd
That tramples my free flowing mind
And narrow me 'til I'm confined
Into a life planned out for me
Where my lost soul is forced to be
Trapped in the dark, destined to dwell
In just another hollow shell

My mirror doesn't tell me lies
It just shows me my dark brown eyes
That steadily return my glare
Compelling me to see what's there
Beyond the skin, the clothes, the hair
And past the plastic smile I wear
Revealing what's now buried deep
Returning while I start to weep
As I reflect on my past years
Discovering through runny tears
That my true self has slowly died
Just leaving emptiness inside
Because I've faded since my youth
When teenage pressure dimmed the truth .

Zachary Ballas
Lawrence High School, Cedarhurst, NY

Unrelinquished Hopes

Before the war, we sung some songs
Celebrating prosperity,
But now we sit and stare, aware,
That no man here is living free.

All was calm and we were fine
In the days of pre-war life.
We enjoyed the little things,
Pleasantly avoiding strife.

It all commenced that fateful day
When they sailed in with flags raised high,
Deceiving they were friend, not foe;
We should have seen through all the lies.

Then accepted, but now spurned,
They advanced upon our land
Laying waste to all they could,
Leaving this place much less grand.

Their army marched from coast to coast
Making fools out of our defense.
The women screamed, the children cried,
Whilst the men just muttered nonsense.

Losing was our only choice,
For a country that was tame.
Now, as slaves, we are not free;
We are forced to live in shame.

We can't enjoy those little things
In this time when we must bow down.
There is no hope for the future;
We could revolt and steal the crown.

That itself sure is a feat,
Though, I think it can be done.
If we can pull together,
Then war with them could be won.

>>

After that, we'd get our throne back
To whom it rightfully belongs.
All our people would rejoice, and
Once again, we could sing our songs.

The way it was, was perfect;
All things we could do, we did.
In the nearing struggle, all
Victory by them's forbid.

That war would be arduous, but
In the end we, we'd reign supreme.
How astounding that would be;
Too bad, for now, it stays a dream.

~ ~ ~

Sarah Berryhill
Freeport High School, Freeport, NY

She is Not Me

She seems so timid and shy
She comes and goes and flits without a word
She leaves soft footprints
Impressed upon me and others
Through me she peeks through the cracks
And sees what goes on and happens around me
But I am her vessel
Bold, outgoing, always alert
I protect her
But sometimes my guard goes down
And she takes over in that quiet
Curious way of hers
I am different
She is not me.
But then I awaken and brush her aside
Being so much younger than I
I wonder why she doesn't cry.
She sits back and seems to abide
By my rules
Yet, every so often in my consciousness,

> >

She tugs at my earlobe with big hoop earrings,
The hem of my
Tight shirt
And points
I can not
Will not
She won't let me
Ignore her pleas
To help others and do what she tells me
Sometimes when she is asleep
And I am at peace
I wonder why that sweet innocent child
Hides in me and why
She is not me.

~ ~ ~

Danielle Brogna
Sewanhaka High School, Floral Park, NY

Time

Easily our friend
Just as easily our foe
This creature walks among us
Hardly unknown
Its persistently moving hands
Attempt to quell our goals
While its shifty, merciless eyes
Oversee what it controls

Times never gives back
What it forcibly takes away
It devours each second, each hour, each day
Its voice is overbearing
To everyone's dismay
There is no way to escape
For you are its prey.

Matthew Chong
Manhasset High School, Manhasset, NY

Soothsayer

Voices press their tongues against the wall,
damp, bentbluish against the
weight of thinning wicks. Offer a gift,
the stone of a peach or the scurf
of tomorrow.

Heed not the stars:
beauty cracks truth against its jaw
like poppy seeds. Listen to whispers
of insects in amber beads,
the prophets of yesterday.

Miss Havisham by choice;
did the sky not blacken with crows?
Do not wait for promise to scurry into fleshless dirt.
Now look to the east:
a boat of chance sails into morning.

Joseph Dash
Wantagh High School, Wantagh, NY

My Dear Friend, Everest!

Cold from the depths of the hard earth,
The lowly commoner gives birth,
To the triumph that one heart can bring,
To this cold and snowy day of spring.
The snow tumbles down the hill,
Bellowing and ready to kill.
Then the darkness will devour,
Your soul within the hour.
If you touch the snowy grains,
Your hand will feel the many pains,
When your skin turns deathly black,
You know you can't go back.

And yet if you reach the top,
You plop yourself right down.
If you take off your goggle crown,
Your eyes will boil, the sun will spoil,
Your sight within the hour.
For the short time that you're here,
You have surely conquered your fear,
But yet you're still not done.
Now you start on down the slopes,
Do you still have hope?

Your tanks are dry,
You begin to cry,
Your hands are numb,
And yet your body hums:
"Get me down you wretched fool!
This is no place to be!
Far too late is it for you to really, truly see.
I'm cold, I'm hot and I'm nearly dead,
Can't I just lie in this snowy bed?"

You calm yourself,
You take deep breaths,
Your heart just skipped a beat.
You light a fire, the smoke goes higher,

>>

And you can feel the heat.
As you see the fire pit,
New hope in you is relit.
As you tread on down the path,
Mother Nature shares her wrath.
And when you have finally made the journey,
Your heart leaps with glee!
You've made the climb,
And you're not blind,
Your skin is peachy pink.
That white darkness has not devoured,
Your soul within that hour!
See? Look at that! You made it!
There's no such thing to fear!
Now a well respected man,
As judgment day grows near.
So go, rejoice, and celebrate!
For you have changed your fate.
As this triumph clearly shows,
Great friends are made from cold hard foes.

Michael DiNunzio
Massapequa High School, Massapequa, NY

Winter

It is a frigid winter day
The air is as crisp as the sea
Which lies before my wondrous eyes

I take a seat on a long, hollow log
Observing my surroundings
While intently examining the world in front of me
I notice a spark of beauty
In the sapphire, blue mist
Gusting into the distance

Even the grass seems peculiar
Losing its verdure from summer's intense blazing sun
Now dull green and hay-like

A sailor heaves the ships (that were drifting merrily in the sea)
Out of their utopia
And hauls them up on the grieving land
They seem saddened for leaving their home
I can hear them sob softly
Saying their goodbyes to the now lonesome ocean

Beyond them are abandoned apartments
Overlooking the lifeless hulls like worried mothers
Then the man who welcomed winter approaches me
He tells me the boat yard is closed for the season
I nod, understanding it is time to go
I take one last glimpse at the deserted area
Thinking of the joys of summer, lingering in my memory

Sarah Anne Dorfman
West Hempstead High School, West Hempstead, NY

Life's a virtue and a sin.
A virtue that is taken for granted.
A sin that's too often committed.
It's the way we try to understand the impossible and the way
we try to make the impossible possible.
Life is about finding meaning in the meaningless.
Noticing things that no one else will notice.
Life is how we try to express ourselves but the truth is so hard to find.
Our job is to expose the truth, and yet we let the lies be told.
It's about hearing words when they don't exist and telling a
story that no one really knows.
Reaching for the stars when you know they're out of reach.
Feeling the sun when there is none.
It's trying to move something you know can't be moved.
Is trying but failing worse than failing to try?
Loving someone who cannot love you but never giving up.
To love the feel of someone's warm embrace.
To keep something that has no worth.
What if that worth was better than money?
What if it meant everything to you, would you give that away?
Is it worth it to look for something that's lost when it's not needed?
Seeing what isn't there and imagining what no one else can.
Caring for the uncared just to see them smile.
Doing what's right even when it's not what you want.
Life's about dreams and how we make them come true.
So dream with no limitations.
Filling in the blanks of life with your own soundtrack.
Because only you can make it what you want it to be.
To make the world different you must change yourself.
To be different you must be you.

Passion is the way we allow ourselves to feel.
A feeling that only we can control.
The way we can see the light, the dark, and in between.
It's the way we live and the way we deceive.
Passion is a heart flamed desire subjective to our inner darkness.
Love is the light that controls our passion.
The force that keeps our hearts from beating out of our chests.
The world is different through everyone's eyes.

I chose the light yet I see the dark and the in between.
The pain people cause because they feel the need.
It's human nature to deceive and yet we still hide the truth in the walls
we build to protect ourselves.
If it's true that people want to be seen, want to be heard, then why
are we still hiding what we all feel?
To change the way we see the world we must change the way
the world sees us.

~ ~ ~

Jennifer Kramer
Great Neck North High School, Great Neck, NY

Dakarai

"Dah-kaaah-rye."
The receptionist scanned the waiting room.
"Dah-kaaah-rye, the doctor is ready for you."
The lanky man put down the Boys' Life magazine,
the one he had clutched distraughtly in his left hand.
His fingers had created crinkles across the forehead of the smiling boy
            on the cover.
It was too early for wrinkles.
The boy looked about nine. Dakarai was thirty-four.
It was too early.

"Dakarai, hello." The doctor reached out to shake the lanky man's hand.
Dakarai tried to read his expression,
but was unable to distinguish if the forehead lines indicated concern
or if they were simply a mark of age.
Dakarai returned the handshake, his mind fixating on the
series of train tracks above the doctor's blue-green eyes.

The doctor confirmed what Dakarai had feared was true,
and when he left the dimmed office forty-five minutes later,
a part of him still did not believe the diagnosis.
Without realizing where his train of thoughts was leading him,
he considered his visit to Zimbabwe three months earlier.
Three months from now, he would be…
Well, he preferred to think about three months in the past.

>>

166

Dakarai had stood by the Mwenezi River,
watching the sun climb higher and higher into the sky
as his mother shared stories about his heritage.
"Dakarai," she would say. "Happiness. Dakarai is happiness."
He would smile and nod and say, "Yes."
His identity and his name had always been intertwined;
he had assumed they always would be.

His name implied optimism, and the more he thought about this,
the more he saw his identity floating out of reach.
Sometimes the situation was surreal, but he knew reality would always hit.
He would feel the same sense of shock.
He would be angry or dismal or bitter, and it was in these struggling moments
he would try to hope.

2,191 hours left. The train would go on, but what would be next?
His name had never been so close to his heart.

Billy Reavy
Herricks High School, New Hyde Park, NY

My heart's beating fast, it's unstable,
Look at you,
you're a satellite dish,
Me? basic cable
            Met you on a hot July day,
But when i was with you girl
i felt as comfortable as if it was May,
            Alright, with this poem i had enough,
if you want to hear the rest of that now,
all i can say to you is tough
            But to my despair,
i have to read to the class, like everyone else,
gotta be fair
            My mind is racing, i don't know where this poem should go,
My teacher is making me write this
Weatherman wrongly said it was gonna snow,
            Maybe i should make a haiku
Nah those are too boring, besides writing poems?
i really don't want to.
            Maybe just stare blankly at this screen, you know? pretend to work
but Mr. Imondi walks around too much
Behind my shoulder he lurks
Maybe i should try a justapowhatmicallit
dang now where can i go with this? Nothin rhymes?
i got a penny and two nickels in my wallet
            Hey this poetry stuff is easier than i thought
here i was thinking,
that i would be caught
            Now i'm just typing away
Oh boy,
i wonder what the class is gonna say
            Will they say that this definitely ain't no bummer?
or that in this last minute
i've just made everyone dumber?
            Will they laugh and enjoy without a care?
or while i'm reading this will they sharpen their pitchforks,
imagining throwing me out the window and through the air?

                                                >>

Well no matter it's too late, maybe i should glance up and see?
have all their stares baring down on me
will their faces be filled with that of gloom or that of glee?

But i don't worry, i have no fear
because in just a minute,
someone else is gonna be up here

Sasha Thomas
Freeport High School, Freeport, NY

Untitled

Promised Land that was never ours to claim
Mothers raped and Fathers maimed
Dreams broken
Hopes dashed
They always prayed these times wouldn't last
These are my people
Whose blood feed this land
Yet a new generation has come along
Ready to stand
Be accounted for
Matter in society
We're in a place that we don't belong
But standing together we will remain strong
Gone were the days with the whips and chains
Gone were the nights of the KKK and all they trained
See, we make progress but we're not there yet
You think racism is gone? Come on
Let's make a bet
Why is it you're only here because of Affirmative Action?
And why was it so hard for Obama to win?
We make believe we are all equal
Seems like our past is coming back like a sequel
They say "so go back where you belong"
How can we when the United States is our home?
Let's get our minds together
Let's write a book
Maybe then the younger generation can see what it took
Freedom doesn't come easy
But my Grams never thought it would be this hard
I'm here to make it better
Stand up for what I believe
For change is in the air and it is definitely a need
I'm not Martin, I'm not Malcolm, I'm not Rosa, and I'm not Harriet
I'm Sasha
And I may have not done anything yet
But believe, and you will see my name will go down in
History

Alisha Tricarico
Oceanside High School, Oceanside, NY

Back In Time

Can I be young again
Go back to the times when
Fairy tales I dreamt were real
And all the pain I felt would heal
Because the only hard times that we had
Is when our siblings got us mad
And the only time we were annoyed
Is when our paintings got destroyed
But now I'm older and times got hard
My heart is played out like a card
And the pain I feel won't go away
And some of my days are just spent to pray
To wish that I can be young again
And go back to the times when
Fairy tales I dreamt were real
And all the pain I felt would heal

12TH GRADE

Stephanie Wang
Roslyn High School, Roslyn Heights, NY

Deep Sea Fishing

The books caught me while I was reading, their slimy, jellyfish ribbons
encasing my fishing pole and wrists like rubber hooks,
slip, slide, grab, trap. The flimsy rowboat is rocked by the waves.

Sylvia Plath would giggle at my predicament,
would offer to pour fire over my tentacle-chains
but would ultimately restrain herself and let me suffer from the pull;
her fire, her story would be hers alone.

Like the stems of something hideous and growing,
the thin, fleshy wrappings, rooted in the book, swell and tighten
and spiral themselves around my fingers,
urging them in a silent struggle
to keep turning the pages.

The words feed the tentacles, the muscular bars of my cell,
And fleeting thoughts for food, for sleep trip over them, disappearing-
'Lo Sherwood, am I grotesque enough for you?
Sherwood Anderson stares silently back, helmet over his heart.
He is shielded by the gloomy Ohio wood that speaks his name,
a tombstone, a bristling darkness
of what is long past.

Can I speak to you? I ask the tentacles,
but they do not respond, only jerk downwards,
hinting at places deep, motioning towards places where
lightness and darkness are one (where Alice Walker would be at peace)
and loneliness sinks away in the company of it all.

I think I could speak to you, even if you are mouthless,
I say, considering, as I catch a glimpse of Walker in the waves.
Even if you are just pages and jellyfish ribbons,
even if you are just words, I will speak to you without them.

The tentacles tighten, embrace with a fresh strength.
I succumb to the depths.
I got pulled out of the safety of the boat and into the sea.
With eyes wide open, I sink.

Melanie Wiederhold
Sewanhaka High School, Floral Park, NY

Posthumous

it's the same with all of them,
so it is with me

now a silent stone
is all that's left;
now the pen
that bled the soul
is safe inside the grave.
but Now,
Now the phoenix rises
from the ruins
and spreads her tempered wings;
silenced voice sounds again,
shrill and harsh, yet brilliant

so take my crumpled thesis, my shattered verse, my disregarded lines
and recall them to life;
unchain the secrets of my darkness
ignored while I was alive;
find the reason to my madness, the genius misunderstood
through folds of mystery, fault and misery;
find the logic locked deep within my incongruity
and praise the twisted mind

it's amazing–
how the shunned
of one generation
becomes the demigod of the next

what is it
that makes you see the light
only after it is out?

12TH GRADE BRONZE MEDAL AWARD

Megan Scher
Island Trees High School, Levittown, NY

Headlights and Gunshots

We didn't see it coming,
And even if we did, it was simply too late.
The headlights blind us,
We hold our breaths.
It's just like the movies,
Your life flashes before your own two eyes.
The moment of impact,
I cannot remember, but I will never forget.
I close my eyes, my heart starts beating.
There's no time to think,
No time to scream, "HELP!"
I just want to be alive,
Please let us be alive.
It felt like hitting a brick wall,
And it felt like dying.
The sound, like a gunshot, left my ears ringing.
An explosion of airbags fills my lungs with dust.
Finally I open my terrified eyes,
And hold my breath once again.
I'm so afraid to turn to her.
Hoping for the best I turn my head.
A sigh of relief,
Thank God she is all right.
It feels so unreal; it must be a dream,
But it's more like a nightmare.
As I step out of the totaled car,
My legs buckle beneath my body.
Besides bruises there's no physical damage,
But there would forever be damage.
You wouldn't call me lucky,
To have gone through such a tragedy,
But I have never been so lucky,
So lucky that our lives were spared.
So lucky just to be alive.

Nichole Coradini
Island Trees High School, Levittown, NY

1 Missed Call

Frozen, the pathway towards the door yells "STOP!"
Her heart cold as the crisp winter air.
No turning back now;
This is everything she asked for.

Misled by the smile that greets her at the door,
Grabbing her trembling hands, he leads her up the stairs.
Stairway to heaven? More like stairway to hell.
Sins were meant to be forgiven.

Guilt races through her weak veins,
As their clothes dance upon the floor.
Thoughts escalating, body dripping sweat
His reassurance means nothing anymore.

As he grips her sinful flesh,
They're distracted by a sound afar
She looks at her phone; it's her boyfriend...
1 Missed Call.

Jeffrey Debrosse
Freeport High School, Freeport, NY

mirror

In a place where soldiers cry
After losing a patient
And nurses thrive
Off the blood and the anguish
Where balloons are C 4
Children run with grenades
And they frown while they play
Where the deer and the ducks
Hunt humans in trucks
Where a grown woman lies bloody
Laughing.
As an infant dies giving birth to her mom
Run, when you hear the sirens
Your innocence will convict you
Where love will, literally,
Kill you and kill you.
A reflection of our world
Where light hides behind
The man with the gun.
A reflection of me is all I see
Naïve as I brush my teeth
And leave.

Sade Faison
Freeport High School, Freeport, NY

Shadow

As I fall into night's hypnosis
like a fall's leaf careens
      Serene
in swirls of peace
engulfed in a shadow
      Fierce
with eyes that pierce
glowing like the metallic sky
      Mysterious
with a mane of black licorice
rippling like the waves of the ocean
stars exude from my smile, stage light
      Bright
a tongue that can flip graves
propel 3,000 trains
      a poisonous kiss
strapped in an armor of truth
in my back pocket lies a vault
of innocence which holds my heart
      With a super hero humble
like a boulder held inside a rubber band
I plummet into the pool of society
with my melted skeleton
      I bend the rules
slashing through conformity
until I lose all nine lives.

Ashley Hill
Freeport High School, Freeport, NY

Where I'm From

I'm from the streets
talk real loud or not enough
I'm from slavery
picking cotton, being told
what to do and when

I'm from drinking coffee
Every single morning
I'm from church
Ten Commandments and all

I'm from gangs and cliques
If you're not in it then
You are "soft or nothing"

I'm from a single parent
Who raised me and my three brothers alone
I'm from friends
Who help you out the best they can

I'm from teachers
Who care how you do in school
From teachers who
Don't care at all

I'm from wannabes and snobs
I'm from good grades and
Readaholics

I just gave you the basics
But there's more from where
I'm from

Kristen McGeough
Garden City High School, Garden City, NY

Wonderland

Bevies of glitter
Stream down red carpets
Hung in the shadows of evening sky

Broken lemons
Patch themselves together
To be eaten for dinner

The queen of hearts makes her entrance
Through ankles tangled in poison vines
Smiles crack and fill with tea at the sight

The rabbit descends to the moon
And hums a sound as delicate as newborn skin

Echoes linger in the empty chairs
Upside down they thud

Lace ties the visitors down to their thrones
The trees feed off incessant laughter

Stuffed dolls sit
In the corners
Listening in on silent conversations

Melissa Montreuil
New Hyde Park Memorial High School, New Hyde Park, NY

Seven Years

Seven years have passed.
Still, like a vivid recurring dream,
Do I see a real life nightmare.
All I can make out is fear, anger, and hate,
Behind the clouds of smoke and tears.
People running from the monsters of terror,
That seek to put an end to all freedom.

Seven years have passed.
The tears have dried,
But the wounds have yet to be healed.
Without forgiveness, we seek revenge,
But the hole will never be filled.
Nothing can replace bravery, soul and pride.

Seven years have passed.
Mothers still weep;
Husbands and wives are left to remember,
As children are left to wonder.
Without an answer, we pray.

Seven years have passed.
Words are felt, rather than said.
Flags are raised and waved,
In the winds of the valiant and brave.

Seven years have passed.
On this sorrowful September,
We remember.

Susan Ng
New Hyde Park Memorial High School, New Hyde Park, NY

dear self,
do not be afraid.
i see that you have beautiful, bold feathers of rich blues, greens and reds.
i hear the power in your voice and something true in your songs.
i know you have wings that allow you to fly. explore. discover.
but you don't.
instead, you trap yourself in the locked gold cage,
hanging in the sky amidst the clouds.
sure, you are safe from dangers and threats, being confined in your dungeon.
but you will still, never be safe from yourself.
because there will always be a fatal yearning that will continue to haunt your
thoughts. the desire to escape, the desire to discover, explore, fly.
and this will never leave until you learn to grow out of your rehearsals.
to roll off your shoulders that burden you created for yourself.
to remove those chains that keep weighing you down.
to unfasten the straitjacket that you thought you looked good in, and
release yourself into the place you meant to be at.
go chase what you've been looking for, however far it takes you.
flutter your wings into uncharted lands, waiting to be discovered.
and remember to stray away from fear, and regret.
you've lived in them, and you know they are dreadful places.
the key is right next to the cage.
all you have to do is reach, unlock, and release.
then you will be free.
best of luck,
me.

Sunjae Park
Roslyn High School, Roslyn Heights, NY

Twilight

From the blue garden above
A fierce heat of red petals
Obliterates a great creation of West
To nothing but miserable dusts
For no value withstands
The grand finale of life

A shower of grief
Eases the agony of heat
Yet pervades a fear of abandon
On a frontier beyond years
Where no breath of life flows

Color of ambition dries in vain
It withers in the shadow
Without a slightest trace

~ ~ ~

Evangelos Razis
Farmingdale High School, Farmingdale, NY

#17

Before me a patch of green amidst a barren waste
The sky shudders with illness, yet all else is silent
I reach out to lie across the dewy grass
And find relief within this remnant

Emily Rogers
Oceanside High School, Oceanside, NY

Waiting to Blossom

My life is an unopened flower
Not yet felt the nurture of another
Waiting for someone to love and care for me
Someone to grow old with
Until my petals are withered and dry
He will be my sunlight
And with him I will blossom

My life was overtaken by a weed
His leaves intertwined with mine
And he took away my sunlight
Like a cloud before a storm
My petals have opened too early
They do not possess the beauty I hoped for
I long to return to the season of unopened buds

James Warren
Freeport High School, Freeport, NY

After It happened, I found myself
       in an empty train station,
a marginally mold green tone to the air
       coughing, clutching my ribcage
I looked down, to find a book
       a cross imprinted, no, burned into the front cover.

Cue Floodlights

       He wasn't wearing a long flowing
moth-eaten brown wool robe
       nor was his beard touching his collarbone.

          (Michael got it wrong, too
       angels are really brunettes
          and as attractive as Satan's Daughters)

       He was wearing a white button down, and Diesel Jeans
Flip-flops, and a cross belt buckle and matching necklaces
       His hands had small scars in the middle
and his top two buttons were down, a Slim, Sophisticated black tie
looped around his neck.

       He was, coincidentally enough
ironically enough,
       to my humor
smoking a Marlboro Light
       The words, "Got God?" written on the side

and no matter how hard he inhaled, the burning end didn't twitch

       "Looks like you're on Santa's good boy list"
he said, his disheveled hair falling over Tommy Hilfiger sunglasses.
       He reached out to me, hands only a little larger than mine
and If I had known better, without the fog light in my eyes
       I might have thought twice
I was just
       shocked I had died, and gone to the heaven
you don't find in the Books.

Samantha Wong
Sewanhaka High School, Floral Park, NY

Glacial Reality

Cold stares, cold glares.
Could anything more make my blood freeze out?
I can feel the distress burning through their souls,
the abomination oozing through their pores.
All the feelings that have once been harbored are finally shown.
I receive treason for what I do?
For what I preach, for what I practice?
It's my morals and my beliefs.
I yearn to stand up for what I put my faith in.
Yet I have to pay the price for wanting to be bold and not feeble.
Their eyes feel like scalpels and stilettos drilling holes through the core of my
heart. And inside, I'm crying out to the one who holds my life.
The pain, the agony. All silenced on the outside,
but secretly deteriorating the body away in the inside.
All I can do right now
is just walk the narrowing tunnel,
exhaling carbon dioxide to the foggy, damp, cold air.
Staring at what surrounds me,
I feel as if everything I earn will now start to seep through my fingers.
Icicles are clashing against the floor as they drop from the surface above.
My précis of the people from afar through my eyes?
They swallow neglect.
Why must this life be so tragic and not at rest?
Will it always be full of wretchedness?
What is out there for us to live for? Dejection?
Wake up, realize for the first time there's a disparity between dreams and reality.
They can feel the turmoil, sadness, and catastrophe eating through their skin,
gnawing at them to get to the deepest of their flesh.
This ache is simply unbearable.
They're wringing with how uncomfortable it makes them feel.
It's strangling society.
It's forcing them to face their true, darkest emotions,
to dig up the memories of the past they thought they had buried once a decade
ago. It's mangling their hearts into a whole new different light and perspective.

> >

It brings up everything that once was.
Why the things that have just been said will remain a mystery,
lurking in the dark and leaving your mind full of questions and tragedy.
And off I go…
into the pitiful world with the slightest hope,
that it's not just filled with lost psyches
gazing back at me without any apparent glow.

ABOUT MAX

Maxwell Corydon Wheat, Jr. was named the first Poet Laureate of Nassau County in New York State, June 24, 2007 by acclamation of poets gathered at Cedarmere, the Long Island home of the 19th century poet, William Cullen Bryant, in Roslyn Harbor.

Maxwell Corydon Wheat, Jr. is a poet, teacher, and naturalist with more than forty years of diverse literary experience teaching, writing for and editing various magazines and newspapers specializing in poetry and poetry related subjects. He has a BA and an MA in English, and an MS in Education. He has received many awards including an Arts & Literary Award, The Long Island School of Poetry Award, Teacher of the Year Award, and multiple Teacher of Excellence Awards. He is listed in *A Directory of American Poets and Fiction Writers, Inc.*

He taught Junior High and Middle School for twenty-eight years and for seventeen years has done nature writing for *Newsday*. He conducts many programs in Nassau County which include workshops and talks at the Freeport Public Library, Taproot programs in Syosset and Port Washington, workshops at the Hempstead Plains Preserve at Nassau Community College in Garden City, and "You Can Write Poetry," a writing course at the Farmingdale High School. In addition, he conducted poetry reading programs at Cedarmere, and was on the board at the Walt Whitman Birthplace in West Hills to help organize their annual poetry contest for school children.

He has published six collections of poetry and developed a poetry website at **www.maxwellcorydonwheatjr.com** for information on writing and enjoying poetry.

ABOUT THE EDITOR

Judy (J R) Turek is a lifelong resident of Nassau County, a member of the Nassau County Poet Laureate Committee, and Chairperson of the Nassau County Poet Laureate School Poetry Project.

J R began writing poetry at age five. Since then, she continues her writing and has been widely published. She is in her eleventh year as Moderator of the Farmingdale Creative Writing Group. She has been nominated for a Pushcart Prize for Poetry, was awarded the Conklin Prize for Poetry, and has won numerous poetry contests. J R is a very active member of the Long Island poetry community.

She has edited several anthologies of poetry, short stories, and novels. J R is the author of *They Come And They Go*. You can contact her at **purplepoet@optonline.net**

Allbook Books *started in 2002 for the publishing of poetry and other writings that encourage one-world consciousness and respect for various cultures, lifestyles and spiritual traditions. The name honors Uncle Alan who was a kind man and a lover of books.*

To order copies of
YOUNG VOICES, **An Anthology of Poetry by Nassau County Students**,
or to receive a catalogue, or for more information regarding books,
poetry readings, tutorials, apprenticeship, haiku workshops,
the art of Chinese calligraphy, text and graphic layout services,
or for further information:

www.allbook-books.com
mankh@allbook-books.com

Allbook Books
PO Box 562
Selden, NY 11784

*

thanks for reading!